D1118563

A REAL

SOUTHERN COOK

IN HER SAVANNAH KITCHEN

WITHDRAWN

⟩A REAL⟨

SOUTHERN COOK

IN HER SAVANNAH KITCHEN

DORA CHARLES

WITH FRAN MCCULLOUGH

PHOTOGRAPHY BY ROBERT S. COOPER

A RUX MARTIN BOOK

HOUGHTON MIFFLIN HARCOURT

BOSTON · NEW YORK · 2015

Copyright © 2015 by Dora Charles
Photographs copyright © 2015 by Robert S. Cooper

All rights reserved

For information about permission to reproduce selections from this book,
write to Permissions, Houghton Mifflin Harcourt Publishing Company,
215 Park Avenue South, New York, New York 10003.

www.hmhco.com

Library of Congress Cataloging-in-Publication Data
Charles, Dora.
  A real Southern cook : in her Savannah kitchen / Dora Charles ; with
Frances McCullough ; photography by Robert S. Cooper.
      pages cm
  Includes index.
  "A Rux Martin Book."
  ISBN 978-0-544-38768-3 (hardcover) — ISBN 978-0-544-38577-1 (ebook)
  1. Cooking—Georgia—Savannah. 2. Cooking, American—Southern Style.
I. McCullough, Fran, date. II. Cooper, Robert S., date. III. Title.
  TX715.2.S68C487 2015
  641.59758'724—dc23
                    2015010770

Book design by Jennifer K. Beal Davis

Food styling by Erin McDowell
Assisted by Sarah Daniels

Printed in the United States of America
DOW 10 9 8 7 6 5 4 3 2 1

For My Father

contents

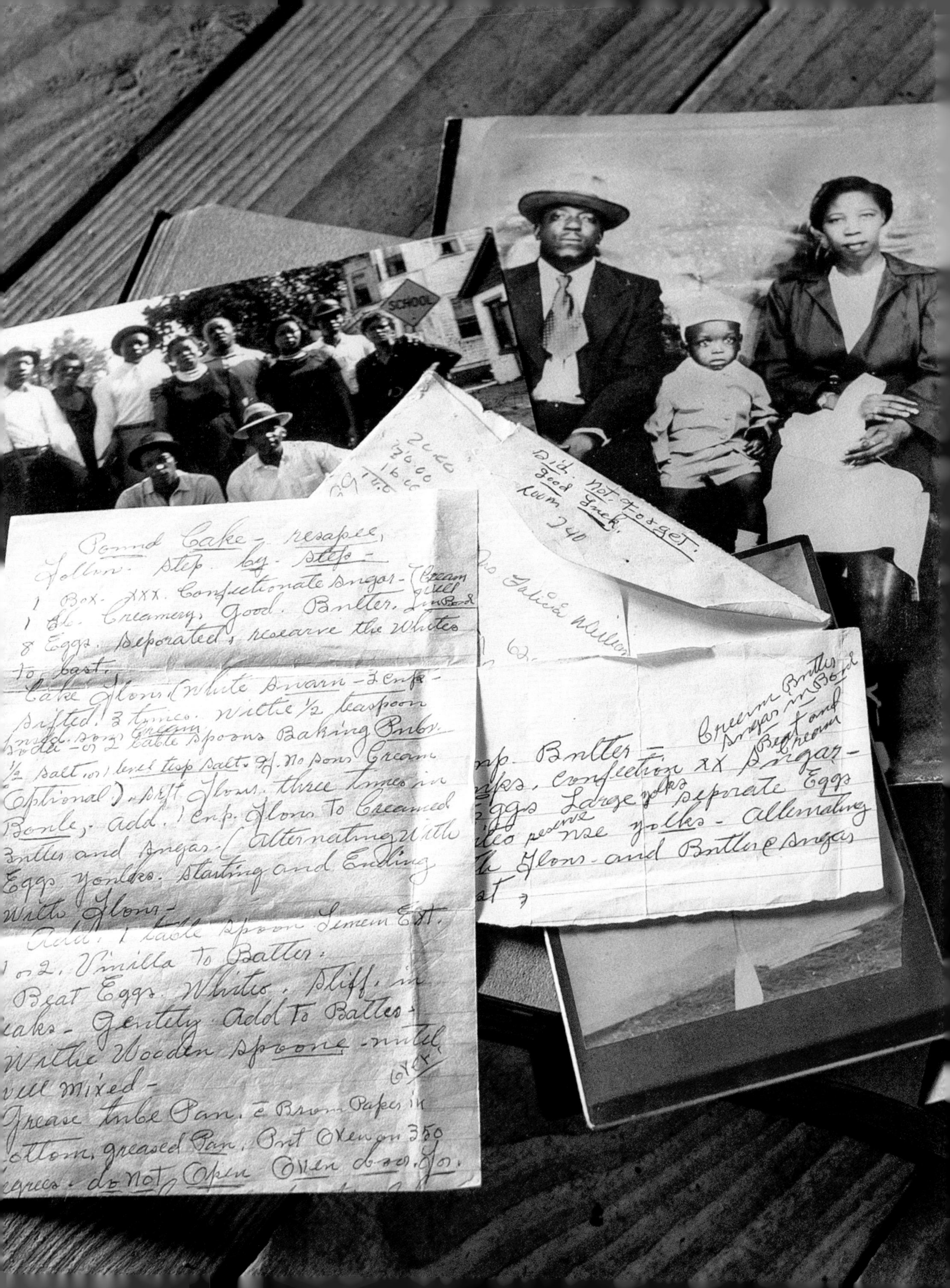

SCHOOL
Pound Cake - resapee,
Follow. Step by. steps -
1 Box. XXX. Confectionate Sugar - Cream
8 Eggs. Seporated, reseave the Whites
to beat.
Beat Eggs. Whites. Stiff. in
Gentely Add to Batter
Grease tube Pan.
Did. Not. Forget.
Good Luck.
room 240

finding my way

THE ONLY MOTHER I EVER KNEW was my grandmother. My mother died when I was just a year and a half old, and my Daddy's mother, a wonderful woman named Hattie Smith, left her home in the country and came to live with us in Savannah. By the time I can first remember things, Daddy was married to my stepmother, Sally—my brother and sister and I called her Sexy—and eventually they lived upstairs in the beautiful Victorian house in Savannah's historic district that he'd been smart enough to buy for $15,000 in the mid-1960s. That house on East Duffy Street had fifteen rooms, which was a good thing, because there was plenty of room for all of us, including Sexy's grown children when they visited and sometimes my half-sisters, Marilyn, Hattie, and Lilliemae, and the half-brothers Skeeter and Thads. Daddy said no one was half of anything and we were all sisters and brothers in the same big family—and he took good care of all of us.

I was the baby in the downstairs family with my grandmother, and I always wanted to be like her. She'd had fifteen children of her own, all born at home—only ten survived—with just a spoonful of corn liquor to get her through the deliveries. She was sweet and kind, but also firm and to the point. She wore an apron all the time and never came out of the downstairs kitchen if she could help it. We ate at her table and were generally her responsibility, even though Daddy was head of the household. She was a church lady, and she didn't play with us, but she did see that we always went to church with her. Sometimes

there were potlucks on special days, and she would bring covered dishes. Those were some eye-popping feasts they laid out. People always looked out for my grandmother's food, and we were proud of her. Everyone knew her fried chicken was the crunchiest on the outside and the juiciest on the inside, with just the right spices to bring it to life. Her baked beans were like no others, so deeply flavored and satisfying they were almost a meal in themselves. And her sweet potato pie was a legend then and still is today, when I make it for all my family and friends at Christmas.

the old days in the country

In fact there was always a fabulously good cook in my family, going right back to slavery, when both sides of my family labored on plantations in the Lowcountry, the coastal area of South Carolina and Georgia. The women were house slaves, so their skills in the kitchen spared them the cruel work in the fields from dawn to dusk. We grew up hearing the stories of slave times, and the tales of the cotton harvest, when my great-grandfather's hands got so tender they'd bleed, stick in my head today—but there was no stopping for pain or blood; you had to keep working until there was no more sun in the sky. The Emancipation Proclamation and, much later, the boll weevil finally put an end to those labors, but the family went on to farm as sharecroppers, working just as hard plowing and growing corn, tomatoes, and peas. Almost all of the crops and the money that came from them—

two thirds—went back to the landowners. My father, who was born in 1918, worked those fields too, and he had to drop out of school before he learned to read or write to help out with the crops.

Only one of my father's nine brothers and sisters survives today, and that's my Aunt Laura, eighty-three years old, who lives in Savannah too. Her stories of growing up on the sharecropping farm are vivid. The farm was in Blackwell, Georgia, about five miles from Monticello, one of the biggest cotton-growing areas in the South.

My family grew cotton, corn, tomatoes, peas, and even cane. They made their own cane syrup—it's the maple syrup of the South. They had two cows and some pigs and chickens. They churned their own butter and made their own lard. They picked their own apples, peaches, and pears and knew where to find all the berries and other wild fruit and nuts. They cured their own bacon and hams. They grew sweet potatoes and white potatoes, peanuts, cabbage, greens of all kinds, carrots, and beans, even lima beans. My grandfather and the boys fished and hunted for ducks, rabbits, squirrels, and possums. A big treat was possum and sweet potato dinner, though Aunt Laura hated it and refused to eat it. The possum would be soaked overnight in vinegar "to take the wildness out of it," and then it would be roasted, surrounded by sweet potatoes.

"There was no stopping for pain or blood; you had to keep working until there was no more sun in the sky."

There was a huge kitchen in the farmhouse, and one year my grandmother canned more than a thousand quart jars from her own garden, so many that my grandfather had to add new wooden shelves up to the ceiling. The water was spring water, lugged up the hill by the children before they went to school or out to the fields in the early mornings. The family was really poor, but the food was so delicious that they often ate like kings. All the sharecroppers helped each other out, traded produce, and shared what they had. Although they could never seem to get ahead, always owing the bosses rent or money for seeds or fertilizer or flour or something else they had to get at the company store, it was a warm community that made its own fun—telling ghost stories, singing, and passing along tales from the old days. Aunt Laura remembers a very old woman who had been a slave coming over sometimes to talk to my grandmother about slave days. Little Laura would run and hide under the bed when she came because she looked like a witch and talked about very scary things, like the story of a child being traded for a pot of cane syrup.

It was a rough life, made even harder by the Depression. The one-room schoolhouse, which had two teachers, was about five miles away, and on Sunday, it became the church. You'd set out on foot at sunrise to get there, and by the time you got home, you couldn't see your hand in front of your face, it was so dark. But they never missed church.

The highlight of the year for the kids was Christmas. My grandparents always made them a nice one, with fruitcake, chocolate cake, nuts, hard candy, raisins on the vine, tangerines, grapefruit, and coconut. There would even be toys—cap pistols and little cars for the six boys, tea sets and dolls for the four girls.

For extra money for the family, Laura and the other children would pick corn and cotton, going to school just a half day on those days. You didn't get any money at all for picking cotton unless you picked at least 100 pounds. Laura was small, so it was hard for her to pick that much, but because the family really needed the money, she'd put a few rocks in if she had to in order to make the weight. Grown men were expected to pick 1,000 pounds a day, women 700 pounds, in the terrible heat and humidity. Even as late as the 1960s, my sister would go out to the country from Savannah to pick cotton for some pocket money. Early in the morning, she'd go to Bull Street, by Forsyth Park, where a truck picked up the workers, and they all rode out in the back of the truck. I would have gone too, except the heat made me headachy and sick, and I'd faint.

My grandmother didn't have a happy childhood. Her mother, like mine, had died when she was a baby, and she was sent to live with a mean

"When I was six, I got bold enough to ask my grandmother to teach me to cook."

aunt. She had two brothers, but they weren't close. Then in 1903, when she was just six, a job for a cook opened up on a farm at a kind of jail, where workers who'd displeased the boss man were kept until they were forgiven and sent back to work. Even though she was a child, she applied for the job, and the old cook taught her how to make the dishes the prisoners ate, three meals a day. That's how she learned to cook.

When she was fourteen, she met and married my grandfather, who was older. He had left his home in Charleston when he was fifteen to become a water boy on the railroad. They moved to Georgia, where my grandfather worked at a fertilizer factory and later on several farms before they settled at the sharecropping farm near Monticello. Neither of them ever got to go to school. Like the other sharecroppers who couldn't read or do arithmetic, they couldn't make heads or tails of the accounting books and so they never knew whether the bosses were cheating them or not.

My father understood that his only hope was to leave the country-farm life. After he married my mother, Pearl Lee Smith, in the 1950s, they had three children, my brother and sister and me, and moved from the country into Savannah. He found a good job in a local sugar factory, but it was hard labor again, since he still couldn't read or write. He convinced Aunt Laura that her future lay in Savannah too, and so she came along. She had the

advantage of having been to school, so she could do all sorts of jobs.

Daddy was a wonderful father to all of us, both his old and new families, and I was always close to him. He liked to say that although he had no education, he had a lot of "mother wit"—and he did. He was smart about almost everything, including buying that fine house. Out of all the ten siblings, Daddy was the one who felt it was his job to take care of his mother, and he was doing that even before my own mother died.

My father liked to take us on family trips, and one of our favorites was to visit Aunt Rosalee, his sister, in Atlanta. She was the great cook of her generation. As soon as breakfast was finished, she'd start cooking lunch—fried chicken, smoth-ered pork chops, cornbread, rice, all sorts of veg-etables, and coleslaw, followed by pies and cakes and cobblers. We'd eat ourselves so full we were sure we couldn't force down any supper, but by the time it was served—the leftovers from lunch, smothered with thickened pan gravy—we could always find a place for it.

Our grandmother would be telling tales of slav-ery days on the plantation, how she still had the flatiron they heated on the wood stove, and how the slaves used to be so terrified of thunder and lightning that they would all gather together in a corner of the house and stay very quiet because "the Lord was doing His work."

Once school was out for the year, my brother and sister and I went to our maternal grandmother's

farm up in Jesup, Georgia, in the central part of the state for the entire summer. We harvested our own watermelons and went berry picking and did chores on the farm. My grandmother took us on roadside picnics, and we had pork and beans, fried chicken, and all the things we still eat today on picnics, like deviled eggs and potato salad. I loved all these times in the country, but even then, at heart I was a city girl, a Savannah girl.

learning to cook on duffy street

When I think back to what I wanted to be when I grew up, it was to be a wife and mother—but with only four children, though my sister had twelve. We would live in our own house and maybe have a garden where I'd grow some vegetables. We'd

have a piano that I would play. The heart of this dream, though, was cooking: I would make great meals that my family would love, just like my grandmother did.

I was always fascinated by cooking and by food itself, how it could be magical in the hands of someone who knew what they were doing and kind of hopeless in the hands of someone else. A good example was living right upstairs. Sexy couldn't cook to save herself, and she'd usually just put a boil pot on the stove, toss in some food, and call it a day.

When I was six, I got bold enough to ask my grandmother to teach me to cook, and she agreed on one condition: First I had to learn to make a proper pot of coffee. She loved her coffee, and as with everything else in her life, she was very

ABOVE: Dora's daughter and grandchildren (*back row*: Keo Charles; Dora; and Dora's daughter, Genie Charles; *front row*: Davion Jones; Brandon Jones; Tay'Shaun Jones; Ja'Kyia Law

particular about it. It had to be Maxwell House, it had to be perked on the stovetop just so, and it had to have just the right amount of condensed milk added to the cup, a special cup with a saucer. It didn't take me long, and then my grandmother pronounced me ready to become a cook. I didn't know then that she too had learned when she was six.

My grandmother learned on a woodstove, using her tiny hands to feel for the proper baking temperature or the right texture for a ball of dough or a meatloaf. She would taste her way to the perfect proportions, and she gave me that great gift. We never measured anything, we just eyeballed it and talked about it and felt it and tasted it until we got it right. We listened for the popping sounds in a pot on the stovetop and adjusted the gas flame accordingly, up or down. She taught me to never waste anything and to save the cooking grease from bacon or fried chicken to flavor something else, like a mess o' greens. We looked to humble cuts like smoked pigs' tails and pork necks to give great flavor to simple vegetables like collards.

I learned to make great fried chicken, juicy inside and crisp outside with no grease on it. My fried cornbread cakes were just right, and my brother loved to eat them with supermarket cane syrup drizzled on top. My sweet potato pie, which we always called "potato pie," got people talking,

"I've taught more than sixty people to cook, but I didn't hand them recipes."

and they still do all these years later. I have to make about fifty potato pies every Christmas or people in the family get very upset.

I've taught more than sixty people to cook, but I didn't hand them recipes. In fact, the ones in this book are the first recipes I've ever written down, except for the large-quantity ones I was asked to write down after fifteen years at Paula Deen's restaurants. Usually I just eyeball the food to death, feel it, and tastetastetaste. My grandmother trained my eyes, my ears, my hands, and my taste buds and taught me to layer in the flavors, and to cook slow, with a lot of love. If you can do that, you really *know* how to cook in your bones, and you're free to cook almost everything— except baked goods, of course. For those you do need a recipe, and you have to be as precise as if you were perking Maxwell House for my grandmother. For this book, I carefully measured every ingredient so I know the recipes will work, but I still urge you to feel and taste everything.

And so it went for six years, as my grandmother passed along her cooking heritage. I was doing a lot of the cooking for our little downstairs family by then, and doing it well. Some people thought I was already grown up, since I looked much older than my age. Sexy had a "liquor house" upstairs, a home bar and lounge where people would come for a drink, maybe the first one of the day, to play cards, and to just have a good time talking and hanging out. I could have a sip or two of bour-bon, and I could play cards. In fact, I was quite the card shark, usually winning games of poker or whist. Sometimes we played for money, and I could count on making some pocket change.

My sisters and brother and I had a little gang of friends—we called ourselves the Duffy Streeters because we all lived on Duffy and somehow it de-fined us. We'd hang out together and sometimes have sleepovers at each others' houses. I wasn't very interested in school, unfortunately, and I loved being out on the streets of Savannah.

And then, with no warning at all, the sun went out. Losing my mother before I knew her was one thing, but losing my beloved grandmother at twelve was com-pletely devastating. It started when she fell coming up the stairs one day lugging some groceries and scraped her shin right down to the bone on one of the steps. My grandmother was light-skinned, and the wound was bright red, really scary looking. The doctors told her that all those years of standing in front of the woodstove, both cooking and warming herself there in the winter, had affected the skin on her legs, and it made the healing very difficult. The gash seemed like it was starting to mend, but then it got infected and that was the beginning of the end—she couldn't be saved. She was only sixty-seven. I didn't know it then, but that was also the end of my childhood, though I was still officially a child.

"At thirteen, I made the biggest mistake of my life."

My father moved me upstairs to cook for the entire family, which was a big job, a grown-up's job. I started feeling like a grown-up, in fact, and I wanted some grown-up privileges, like going out on the exciting streets of Savannah, meeting new people, and having my own life. At thirteen, I made the biggest mistake of my life, falling in-sanely in love with a slightly older man who, of course, turned out to be exactly the wrong person for me. Georgia state law would have protected me from this crazy marriage, but I was so in love, so eager to start my own life, that I convinced Daddy to stand up for me in South Caroli-na, where such early marriages were just fine. I think he would have done almost anything to make me happy at that point, so he put aside his "mother wit" and said yes. We crossed the bridge into South Carolina, and my Daddy gave his permission by signing with his usual *X*. I had gotten what I thought I wanted, but it didn't take me long to realize it wasn't what I wanted at all. Soon there was jealousy, violence, and abuse, and in the end I was lucky to emerge in one piece, though I was a little wiser.

trying my wings

I soon met a sweet man from the Caribbean is-land of St. Lucia who was smart and a jack-of-all-trades—he could fix anything. It was twelve years before we even got married, but by then we had Eugenie, our wonderful daughter, nicknamed Genie. After a while, though, that relationship also soured, and I decided I needed a job to support my daughter and me so I could be responsible for my own happiness.

Because I never finished school, I didn't have a lot of choices. But I could cook, I knew that for sure. I didn't know how you went about becoming a professional cook, but I decided to just go for it. The Days Inn needed a short-order cook to make breakfast at the motel and I was sure I could ace breakfast. Thank God, Martha, the morning cook I was relieving, gave me some important lessons. Pretty soon I got the rhythm, and it was a little like performing onstage, with the hungry people as the audience and me trying to make it all come out perfectly—which, most of the time, it did. I must be part ham, because I loved that feeling of meeting the challenge over and over again and making people happy as they started their days.

"After a while, I got a reputation for my food."

After a while, I got a reputation for my food, and I cooked at a series of clubs and grills. It was while I was working at one of them, Bennigan's, that I met up with a friend of mine who was cooking two nights a week for Paula Deen. He told me Paula was looking for a new chef, and that I should go talk to her. That conversation changed my life. Paula was running the restaurant at Best Western on the south side of Savannah, serving breakfast, lunch, and dinner. The restaurant was called The Bag Lady—and she also had a business with the same name that delivered bag lunches to office workers. We really hit it off when we first met. She'd ask me how I'd cook something in particular, and I'd tell her how my grandmother cooked it, and she'd say that's almost exactly how *her* grandmother cooked it. A lot of people don't realize that Southern country food is pretty much the same for both black people and white people, except most black cooks are more concerned with seasoning. We loved to talk about food, and I liked Paula and liked the fact that she was such a fan of my food. In the beginning, it was just for Mondays, until the job actually opened up. Paula begged me to hang in, because people who came in then were loving the food, and she told me constantly how much she enjoyed it herself. So I did, for about two months.

Once I started full-time, it was a very long day. I would arrive at five o'clock a.m., and Paula would start that early too, stopping off at Kroger's to buy food for the day. It wasn't long before I had my own key, and I opened the place, setting up the grits, starting a sauce for the shrimp and grits, and putting on the chicken for a delicious dish we served then. Paula would be making the bag lunches, and everyone else would stagger in to get the coffee on a little before 6 o'clock a.m., when we opened. Soon the "new" food was attracting

so many people that Paula dropped the bag-lunch business because she didn't have the time for it.

In the beginning, it was just Paula and me in the kitchen, prepping and cooking. Our food was very similar, though she had a gift I didn't have until much later—if we ran out of something, Paula could always put together a delicious meal in a heartbeat from what was left in the refrigerator, but my dishes always had to cook for a long time. We joked, we laughed, we cooked side by side. Soon we had lines out the door because of word of mouth. Paula asked me if I knew anyone who could help us out in the kitchen, and in fact I did. My friend Felicia and I had been exchanging covered dishes for a while, and her husband said mine were so much better than hers, could I teach her how to cook? Before long, he couldn't tell who made a dish, Felicia or me—so I knew Felicia could do what I did. She actually came to us for less pay than she was making at the time because she liked the job so well. And then we needed more help, and my sister came.

In the kitchen, we joked and danced, and Paula really liked to join in on all that. You had to get your work done too, but having a good time made the work go so much faster and brought so much joy to the whole process that it actually made us more efficient. Paula would say, "How do y'all black people know how to clap and snap your fingers and stomp your feet all at the same time? I can't do it, I have two left feet, you have to teach me!" Of course we didn't even know what we were doing, so we couldn't teach her, but she

kept trying hard because she thought it was so cool. We'd laugh and laugh, and then we'd all sit together for a meal and laugh some more. Paula thought it was important to have a happy kitchen, and we certainly had that. If we hadn't been able to joke around, we would have ended up pulling each others' hair out, we worked in such close quarters and under pressure.

Part of the fun was to prank each other, and that included Paula too. She was a great sport, and she'd laugh as much when you played jokes on her as when she got you. She got me good on several occasions, and I returned the favor. It was all part of the good humor in the kitchen—always working hard, but always ready to be playful too.

One day I came out of the bathroom, and she put her arm around my shoulders and walked me around the kitchen, talking and taking me all over to talk to the other people, who would start laughing. She even took me out into the alley, where the staff went on breaks. Finally I said, "Paula, why are you taking me around and why is everybody laughing?" She hooted, "Because, Dora, you have a big old piece of toilet paper hanging out of your pants in the back!" She laughed and laughed, and I couldn't imagine how I had gotten that toilet paper tail.

I had to think about a good payback for that one. One afternoon when Paula was getting anxious about a big catering order, I told her I just hadn't been able to finish it, there wasn't time, and I was really sorry. I thought she'd faint, she got so red in the face and looked like she was about to die, because she was such a perfectionist. Actually I didn't like her asking if I did it—*of course* I did it, I always did. I was a perfectionist too. Then I put on a big grin and she knew.

Paula didn't like to run out of food, and the more people heard about how good the food was, the more people came to the restaurant, and sometimes we did run out. She set up a system: I was supposed to come and tell her in the front of the house when we were on our last tray of chicken so she could go out and get more. One day I did that, and she was so busy helping the servers that she didn't leave. I went up front and told her again. Really she needed a runner to get the chicken, but she was so busy she forgot about it. When we actually did run out, she went to the grocery store and got a big box full of wrapped packages of chicken, and she was so mad that she threw it at my feet, saying, "*Here's* your chicken!"

I was my usual cool self, just standing there, and I was not going to pick up that chicken. I can be very stubborn. Finally a dishwasher came and picked it up, unwrapped it, and cleaned and seasoned it. It wasn't long before Paula came back into the kitchen and apologized, and then we hugged and were back to our usual jokey selves. "How do you do it, Dora?" she said. "I just don't understand how you keep so calm in here—I wish I could be as calm as you." "Oh," I said, "you *don't want* to see me mad in this kitchen . . ."

"We were a good balance, and it really did seem that we were soul sisters."

I could keep calm, but I think Paula's way of letting it all out and then getting over it was actually better—I would keep it all inside and kind of swallow it. Restaurant kitchens are big pressure cookers about to explode, and it's good to let off steam if you can.

For the catering jobs, it was just Paula and me cooking together, sometimes for a hundred and fifty people. We worked so hard and got so much done, we were like partners. Sometimes we'd do the work in her home kitchen if the restaurant kitchen appliances were being fixed. We'd talk about our grandmothers and their cooking while we were working, tell stories and laugh.

One night we were on our way to a Christmas catering job, with Paula and the dishwasher in one car and me in another, and we were not late exactly but not early either. It was dark and raining. I didn't know where we were going, so I had to follow Paula closely. Both our cars were filled with food. She stopped suddenly, and I rear-ended her car, and she rear-ended the car of the man ahead of her. Paula and I both jumped out and started crying. The man Paula hit didn't have any real damage, and he said to just go on, he wasn't even going to report it.

So we went on to the party, but once we were there, we still couldn't stop crying, because the food was thrown all over and by now we were close to being late and the clients were angry.

Finally the dishwasher put his arms around both of us and said, "Please, you have to stop crying, or I'm going to start crying too, and we'll never get this job done." We both dried our eyes and sprang into action. Paula could always dress a gorgeous table, and I couldn't believe how she pulled it off—all this smashed-up food ended up looking like a million dollars after she was done with it, and the clients were so happy.

It was kind of unlike us, because I was always the calm-as-a-cucumber one and Paula was the one who could get upset if things weren't just perfect. We were a good balance that way, and it really did seem, as Paula liked to say, that we were soul sisters, born just a day apart but with such different temperaments. I learned a lesson that night—that you can make anything you're serving look good if you put your mind to it, no matter how much misfortune it's suffered. And whatever's happened, you can always save the day if you stay calm.

People were constantly coming into the restaurant trying to hire me away for two and three times my salary, but I always said no. The only time I said yes was when a man from Denver who had a rib joint there asked me to come out for a quick consulting job to show him how to cook vegetables. His ribs were really good, but his cooks just couldn't get the vegetables right. I showed him a new way to cook them. A few weeks later he called to say that one of his customers had

"Build the flavor and cook it slow so it can bloom."

brought in a baby about three years old who'd never touched a vegetable in his short life, but he ate the entire plate of green beans I'd shown them how to cook, and the parents couldn't get over it.

hitting the big time

Our lines were getting longer and longer at The Bag Lady, and the hotel started complaining when they reached out into the lobby. Paula was ready for a bigger restaurant anyway, and she wanted to be right downtown. She asked me to come with her. Of course I said yes. I loved what I was doing, and I loved working with Paula. She had big ambitions, and she was very good at marketing the whole mystique about down-home Southern food. She told me I was a big part of the plan. Holding my hands and looking deep into my eyes, she said, "Dora—(she always pronounced it *Doe*-ra in her deep Southern accent)—if I get rich, you get rich." I never got rich in financial terms, but I got rich in many other ways.

We were cooking the kind of food I loved, real Southern cooking, twelve hours a day and six days a week. It was constant hard work, but to my surprise, I found I really loved working so hard; it made things more interesting. I hadn't done that before, day in and day out, but it was a challenge that I prided myself on meeting, and it gave me a lot of satisfaction. We dropped breakfast at The Lady & Sons, the name of the new downtown restaurant, so we could come in at eight in the

morning, but the machines broke so often that we would have to do it all by hand, so I suggested we all come in at six o'clock. And that's what happens to this day at Paula's restaurant.

Back when we were at Best Western, Paula had the idea of asking the customers for their favorite family recipes, and she put out cards at the table to encourage them. She was planning to publish a cookbook, and a lot of those recipes, or some version of them, ended up in the book, including one of mine for baked spaghetti. That was the first cookbook I ever owned. People bought the book and talked about it, and that brought even more people to the restaurant.

I was not only cooking but also teaching other people how to do it. I kept to my grandmother's

ideas: Build the flavor and cook it slow so it can bloom. Put the love into it and pay attention—that care you take with it is what will make it delicious. It's hard to do that when you're cooking for so many people and you don't have total control over every step of the way, but if you're watching out for the quality, you can make it happen. At Paula's restaurant and at her brother's place, Bubba's, I trained two of the dishwashers to become excellent cooks, and they later became managers.

There were certain things I wouldn't do. Paula came in one day all excited about a new plan to announce that the restaurant was now open for lunch. She wanted me to come out in front of the restaurant and ring a loud bell. No way would I do that. Then she wanted Jellyroll, another longtime cook, to dress up in an Aunt Jemima getup and ring the bell. In the end, Jellyroll agreed to ring it, but with no Aunt Jemima outfit. When we moved up the street much later, Paula wanted Jellyroll to make hoecakes right in the middle of the restaurant, dressed up like Aunt Jemima. Jellyroll wouldn't go for that either, though she had exactly the right old-fashioned look Paula wanted.

Soon we had so many customers that we couldn't accommodate them all in that small restaurant, so we moved up the street to a big corner building where The Lady & Sons is today. We could serve up to fifteen hundred people a day, eighteen at holidays, plus constant catering clients. Those were the numbers they came up with at the front of the house, where they were counting heads, but in the kitchen, we counted plates, because people could return to the buffet two and three times with a new plate, and they often did, piling them up. It felt like we were cooking for thousands and thousands of people, but we didn't even think about it, we just did it. We now had six cooks plus prep people, but we were still working just as hard as before. We had giant pots of food on the stovetop, and we had to stir them with a sort of boat paddle, so we had to be strong.

Paula had her family, her sons helping out in the front of the house, and I had my family and friends in the kitchen. I wasn't doing the hiring, but in fact I brought in most of the cooks—my

"Country people in the South had to make do with what was at hand."

sister, my nephews, my best friend—and that was one reason we all worked together so well. The management had hoped that I would do the firing, but I said if I do the firing, I do the hiring. If you do the hiring, you do the firing.

Paula was getting famous, although a piece of her heart was always in the kitchen and she'd still come in to cook with us when she could. Once she started appearing on QVC, though, she was often out of town, and we had no idea whether she was in Savannah or not. One day we were looking for her and asked where she was and were told she was on a cruise, a Paula Deen cruise. Jellyroll said, "Huh, why doesn't she take us along on those cruises?" The next time she saw Paula, Jellyroll proposed the idea, and Paula really liked it.

When Paula became a national celebrity, things at the restaurant started to change. But to me, she wasn't a star, she was my old partner. Bobby and Jamie, who used to give me a hug and a kiss as they went by, got much busier, though they were there all the time now. I had become a manager, at $18 an hour instead of $10, but things were not the same.

There were lots of little things and a few big things that caused me to choose another path and leave my job of twenty-two years. When I did leave, it made some news—not good news to everyone, but leaving was good for me. It took me a while to see that God had opened a door for me, not closed one, and I could stand tall and walk through it. Once I understood that, I promised myself that I wouldn't walk back through that door, even just in my mind. I wouldn't mull it over and over or even talk about the bad times. And I keep that promise to this day.

I also realized that what I'd always wanted to do was share the food I'd learned to cook at my grandmother's hands, the food I think of as true Southern cooking—not fancy city cooking, but the kind we have been doing for a very long time. And in the process of putting together the book, I learned a lot about my family, our history, and how we all got to this point in this place, my beloved Savannah.

good southern country food

A lot of people have a kind of *Gone with the Wind* picture of Southern cooking. In their heads, there's a huge candelabra and a planter's table set with fine linens and silver and piled with platter after platter of the best food you could ever imagine. A feast every day. My great-grandmother was probably in the kitchen at some of those feasts, and she may have known a bit about how to prepare them, but that old planter's table really is gone with the wind.

Real Southern country food is a feast, but it's one based on flavor and knowing how to coax flavor out of everything you can and serving plenty of it. It's more elaborate than soul food, though the Lord knows it can wake your soul right up with its deep, satisfying tastes, the kind only home cooking can give you. That feast might be a fantastic breakfast, with shrimp and grits, sausage and eggs, chicken, biscuits and white gravy, baked beans, omelets, coffee cake, banana nut bread, and blueberry or blackberry muffins—some of it or most of it. For holidays, there have to be certain things like potato salad, even for Christmas. There will also be collard greens and ham, fried chicken, mac and cheese, sweet potato pie, and banana pudding and sour cream chocolate pound cake—at the minimum.

We didn't always have those feasts. Country people in the South had to make do with what was at hand, what they could grow or trade or preserve. There wasn't a grocery store a few blocks away so they'd have to use their mother wit to feed themselves well. Country people eat rice on and under everything, partly because we're in the Lowcountry, where rice is serious business, but I think also because rice keeps forever and you don't have to worry about running out to get more all the time. Aunt Laura tells a story about the tea cakes—shortbread cookies—at my grandmother's house in the old days. They'd wash a flour sack and dry it in the sun, then put those cookies in the sack and hang it from the ceiling, safe from little children's hands—so they'd always have a little something sweet to eat.

I don't have to tell you that the original makedo cooks in the South were slaves. I've been told that a field worker's food rations for a week on a cotton plantation like the one where my great-grandfather harvested cotton were just a few

ears of dried corn and three pounds of fatback or sidemeat. They grated the corn and mixed it with water to make a meal of cornmeal mush, or they made hoecakes right on the flat part of the hoe over a fire, greasing it with a little fat from the fatback. That and whatever green things they could harvest or grow would be it for the week. There might be some eggs or a peach found growing off by the river, but mostly it was the same all the time. Yet those tastes are still what we crave: cornbread, bacon, greens. They speak to us, black and white alike. Cooked right, they sing a powerful song.

Someone from up North asked me once if I thought there was a difference between black Southern food and white Southern food. I said yes, and then I had to think a minute. Finally I said the difference is that black Southern food is just bursting with flavor. It's the seasoning that sets it apart. It doesn't matter how humble your food is, you can always bring up the flavor that's lurking there. To this day, we know the value of smoked turkey neck, pigs' feet, and all those little bits that give you much more flavor than their very small cost. Even some canned peas or beans, if you cook them long enough and season them carefully enough, will have people who eat them swearing you were out in the kitchen shucking peas or snapping beans all day long, they taste that good.

A lot of people in my family and among my friends think leftovers can be much better

"Black Southern food is just bursting with flavor."

than fresh-cooked food, especially dishes like Next-Day Fried Greens and Rice (page 69). My grandfather loved to eat leftover cornbread with buttermilk and also with greens. The edges of the cornbread get dried out, yes, but that just means it's ready to take up the juices of whatever you're dipping it in, or to be turned into the basis of a delicious stuffing. Leftover chicken or pork smothered in gravy has all the flavor of the original dish, plus more from the gravy.

My grandmother always added a pinch of sugar to tomatoes, peas, and beans, especially limas, if she hadn't soaked them. She grew most of her own vegetables on the farm, and when she moved to Savannah to take care of us, my father would go to City Market, the farmers' market downtown, to buy fresh produce to bag and freeze what wasn't eaten that day and the next. We children loved the vegetables just as much as every other part of the meal. Of course you have to know how to choose only the freshest ones at the market, how to treat them, how to cut up collards before you cook them. People are always asking me where my recipes come from, and my usual answer is: my grandmother. Because of her, I learned recipes the way they were cooking them in the early 1900s here in the country. We didn't even write them down, we just learned how to do it, how food works.

But the way people cook changes all the time and even the basic ingredients, like real buttermilk and real rendered lard, change. I don't just make old-timey food. Like everyone else, I fell in love with Italian food at some point, and I always have pasta and a bottle of good olive oil in my kitchen. I get cravings for the flavors of Mexican food, so I have cumin and chipotle pepper in my spice cabinet. And I love Spanish smoked paprika, which goes so well with our own Southern food.

When I lived in Pennsylvania for several years, I had to shop in markets so unlike the ones in Savannah that sometimes I wondered what there was to eat there. That's where I discovered kielbasa. Key limes were all around me in Savannah, but I didn't discover them until fairly recently. Now I love to squeeze them over watermelon or cantaloupe or just make fresh limeade with them.

I have an extended family of nearly a hundred people, all enthusiastic eaters and cooks. We love to get together and cook, and we're always trading recipes. I love to try new recipes, and I can almost never restrain myself from playing with them a bit. So these are mainly family recipes, country Southern recipes, with some newer ones too.

We have a saying down here for when you throw your whole heart and soul into something— we call that "putting your foot in it." And when you put your foot in it and work with the flavors to take them to the next level and season everything and taste constantly to be sure you have it right, that's the special touch of Southern food.

I love the moment when everyone comes to the table and their eyes are all lit up with anticipation. We always say a blessing then, because we *are* blessed and we ask for the food to be blessed too. I see this food as a tribute to those who came before me, who worked so incredibly hard for so little. When you're very poor, with no hope of moving out of it, your wealth is your family. For the cook, there's nothing quite so joyous as seeing your family and friends gathered around a big table, loving all the dishes you've made for them, telling stories, keeping older traditions, and making new ones. That's what I want to share with you in this book—especially the younger generations who are losing the connection with home-cooked food and why it's important. There really *is* a joy in cooking. If you don't cook real food, you have no idea of the great pleasure that's waiting for you when you do—the cooking itself, the tasting, the sharing, the passing along.

morning food

MY FIRST JOB COOKING was as a short-order cook at Daybreak, the breakfast restaurant at the Days Inn in Savannah. I knew I could cook, and I knew there was a job open, so I just presented myself, said I could do it, and got the job. I was scared to death, because I was cooking right in front of people, and I had to do it fast and do it right. About a hundred people came in every morning with very particular ideas of how their eggs and everything else should be done. I was whirling around, flying from griddle to pan, and turning out sausages, bacon, grits, eggs, pancakes, waffles, whatever anyone wanted.

I had some help from Martha, the morning cook I was replacing, who became a really good friend. Martha got me over the hump. It didn't take me long to get the hang of it, though, and once I did, I just loved it, loved the challenge of it and loved making people happy with their food. I couldn't believe what some people were asking for, things like just egg whites, cooked so that they were barely warm. But I pulled it off, and I felt great about it.

I'm fussy about my eggs too. I love breakfast, and I especially love an egg cooked over-medium, just right. I've never found anyone else who could do this perfectly except my daughter, who I trained the way my grandmother trained me. I hate it when you ask for over-medium and you get over-easy. With that one, the minute I put my fork into the yolk, I feel like I'm in a race with that egg, that it's trying to beat me to the white line of the grits, it's so runny. The

over-medium egg yolk is still a bit runny but it's thicker, like a sauce, so you can take a forkful of your grits before the yolk makes its way toward the grits.

It was working in that tough environment so happily that made me think I really *was* born to cook, that I could make it the work of my life. And I still love breakfast. Best of all is a big spread, with country ham, bacon, sausage, grits, eggs, biscuits, fresh fruit, shrimp and grits, waffles or fried cornbread with cane syrup drizzled over, fried apples, and maybe something fancy like a croissant. It's one of my favorite feasts and a wonderful way to start a special day.

Because I love breakfast so much, my daughter, Genie, makes me a knockout one each year on the morning of my birthday, and there are always surprises, treats I've never tasted before, joined by old favorites. I think Christmas morning should also be a special breakfast time, a great way to start a day so full of blessings. Aunt Laura had a recipe in her files that came from a coworker many years ago; it's for the famous cinnamon rolls this woman made for Christmas morning. The aroma of fresh cinnamon rolls in the oven is unbeatable—or, if that seems a little too ambitious, or if working with yeast scares you, make my Huffy-Puffy Oven Pancake to give your family the same kind of experience.

Breakfast is usually for family or close friends—it's just by nature an intimate meal to be shared with people you love. It doesn't have to take a long time. You can have overnight grits ready the minute you get up, and all by itself that will make breakfast special even on a weekday. Add bacon or sausage, eggs, and maybe some banana bread you made the day before, and you're all set for a great day.

I wouldn't be my Grandmother Hattie's granddaughter if I didn't also say you need to give the people at your table a really good cup of coffee. That's the magical ingredient that makes breakfast work, something I've known since I was four years old.

down-home country grits

You dare not serve anyone in the South breakfast without some well-cooked grits. Now that grits are on plates all over the country, people get into fights about them— they have to be white or they have to be yellow; they have to be stone-ground, which means coarse, or they have to be fine-ground, like quick-cooking grits; they have to be cooked a long time, or hardly at all.

You know I have my own ideas. I love the delicate taste of white grits, and I like the fineness of quick-cooking grits. But I don't use quick-cooking grits to save time; I cook them for about an hour, slowly and gently, stirring, so they're creamy and rich. Stone-ground grits, to me, taste too "gritty," but if you like them, you cook them the same way. I also have an overnight version for those grits that gives them a really smooth texture (page 38). You should try it.

Grits are not only for breakfast. They're often served as a side dish with dinner, and of course Shrimp and Grits (page 72) is one of the great dishes of my part of the South. But because breakfast is unthinkable without them, I've put the recipe here.

My family and friends and I all rinse grits three times—a little of the starch comes off, and I think they taste better. SERVES 4

1. Put the grits in the large saucepan you plan to cook them in. Fill the pan halfway with hot water, swish the grits around a little, let them settle to the bottom, and pour off the water; repeat two more times. On the third and final rinse, tip the pan slowly and carefully, holding the grits back with your hand, and pour off as much of the water as you can without losing the heavier grits—it's fine if the lighter grits float up and go down the drain.

2. Add the 5 cups hot water to the rinsed grits and stir with a whisk. Add the salt. Cover the pan and bring to a boil over medium heat. Lift the lid to stir often, and watch that the pan doesn't boil over. As you stir the grits, you'll notice that after 15 to 20 minutes they will suddenly start jumping around and making a popping sound; this means that the water is disappearing. Then it's time to turn the heat down a little, to

1⅓ cups quick-cooking white grits

5 cups hot water

½ teaspoon salt, or more to taste

2 tablespoons butter

Ground black pepper to taste (optional)

medium-low, and leave the grits to simmer. Keep the lid on and, from time to time, give them a good stir.

3. After the grits have cooked for an hour, stir in the butter. Taste the grits for salt and add more if you need to, as well as the pepper, if you're using it. Serve right away, or cover and keep the grits warm on the stovetop over low heat. Stir them every now and then and check to see if you need to add a little more hot water. They'll keep for hours this way.

TIPS

• Fill the grits pan with hot water the minute you're done serving them, and by the time you're finished with the rest of the dishes, the pan will be ready to clean easily.

• For cheese grits, I just add a handful or two of shredded cheddar cheese to the hot grits and stir it in well.

• We kids used to make grits sandwiches for breakfast, and I taught my grandsons how to make them too. Take some soft bread—these sandwiches are supposed to be squishy—and hook up your hot grits, as we say, with cheese and butter and salt and pepper or whatever you like, then spread a layer of them on top of a slice. Enjoy open-face, or top with a second slice of bread, or just fold the bread over. None of us ever left the table hungry.

overnight stone-ground grits

I'm not usually crazy about stone-ground grits because they don't have that silky quality I like so much, but these are an exception to my rule. In the long, slow, overnight cooking, they develop a smooth texture that's really good. Plus, you can't beat the convenience of putting them in the pot, setting them in the oven for the night, and opening the pot in the morning with your perfectly cooked grits all ready to go.

Just be sure you have real stone-ground grits from a mill (see Sources, page 263) and keep them in the freezer so they'll be fresh. If you have an electric oven (most gas ovens won't go low enough) and a pot with a tight-fitting lid—a Dutch oven is fine—you're all set. The idea is to mix water and grits in a ratio of 4 to 1, with a little salt. You can make as much or as little as you want, but here's a starter recipe.

SERVES 4 TO 6

1. Start the night before: Set the oven to 180 degrees—usually the lowest setting.

2. In a pot with a tight-fitting lid, stir together the grits, water, and salt. Cover the pot and slide it into the oven to cook undisturbed overnight.

3. The next morning, taste the grits—they might need more salt. I like to add pepper and butter too, before serving them hot.

1 cup stone-ground grits

4 cups water

1 teaspoon salt, or more to taste

Ground black pepper to taste

About 2 tablespoons butter, for serving

> **TIP**
>
> Leftover grits are no problem. Make grits cakes (see photo opposite)! Spread them out in an even layer in a shallow pan and let them cool completely, or refrigerate, covered, overnight. Spread a hot griddle or skillet with bacon grease or butter and cut the grits into shapes: squares, circles, triangles, whatever. When the grease is hot, add the grits cakes and cook over medium heat, turning once, until golden brown and crispy on both sides. Grits cakes are great for breakfast or as a side dish.

> **TIP**
>
> If you like real old-fashioned Irish steel-cut oatmeal, you can cook it exactly the same way and it will be ready for breakfast when you get up in the morning. Add some raisins and cinnamon, and you have a great winter morning breakfast.

change-your-life stewed salmon with grits

I remember my grandmother making this dish often, either for breakfast over grits or for dinner over rice. I'm not sure how it got started, but on Fridays we'd often have fish and grits. It was a quick dinner you could make out of things you usually had in the cupboard or the refrigerator, and everyone loved it.

I served it one morning to my great-nephew, Greg, and he started to pick out the green pepper. Then he gave up on that and ate it all with great enthusiasm. "This is really good!" he said. He told me that his entire life he'd picked out green pepper and onion bits from any food he was served—he just thought he didn't like them. But now he loves them. That's how this dish got its name. SERVES 4

1. Fry the bacon in a large skillet until crisp. Drain the bacon on paper towels; save the bacon fat and wipe the crumbs out of the pan with a paper towel.

2. Add 1 tablespoon of the bacon fat back to the skillet, along with the butter, and heat over medium heat until sizzling. Cook the green pepper and onion, stirring once or twice, until they're limp. Add the salmon and the salmon juice, breaking up the salmon a little but not too much—there should still be some distinct pieces. Add the seasonings and let the salmon simmer for 5 to 10 minutes.

3. Put the hot salmon right in the middle of a pile of grits or rice. Crumble the bacon into generous pieces and sprinkle it over the grits or rice. Garnish the whole dish with the parsley and serve.

5 bacon slices

2 tablespoons butter

½ cup diced green bell pepper

½ cup diced onions

1 (14.75-ounce) can pink Alaska salmon, picked over to remove skin and bones; save the juice

½ teaspoon salt

½ teaspoon ground black pepper

½ teaspoon Accent (optional)

Grits or rice, for serving

1 tablespoon chopped fresh parsley, for garnish

talking about cast-iron skillets

I have a secret weapon in the kitchen: It's my grandmother's old cast-iron skillet with a glass lid. It seems to glow with all the wonderful food she cooked in it over the years. When Southerners talk about cast-iron cooking utensils being seasoned, that's what we really mean—that they've absorbed a little of the flavor of decades of cooking, and they give it back to us when we cook in them. My grandmother's skillet has a surface that's almost soft, so it's naturally nonstick. Cast iron holds heat like no other cookware, giving you a great crust on your cornbread or crisp edges on your sausage patties and your fried fish. It's really the signature of Southern cooking—you see an old iron skillet or Dutch oven on the stovetop, and you know you're in for some wonderful food.

It takes just a little bit of maintenance to keep your skillet going. You can buy preseasoned skillets, but I like to do it myself, and reseason it from time to time if it starts to lose that glow.

TO SEASON OR RESEASON A SKILLET

Wash the skillet well in hot soapy water and dry it over medium heat on the stovetop. Set the oven to 375 degrees. Spread a thin layer of grease all over the skillet—it can be lard, Crisco, or just vegetable oil. Put the skillet in the oven for an hour, then turn off the oven and leave the skillet in there to cool down. Wipe it out with paper towels when it's cool. If it's very humid at your house, store the skillet in a brown paper bag to absorb any extra moisture, which will keep it from rusting.

MAINTAINING YOUR SKILLET

Always put a little oil or bacon grease in the skillet before you start cooking. The naturally nonstick surface doesn't mean that you shouldn't use any fat in the pan; it just means the food won't stick if you treat the skillet properly.

Try not to use more than a little soap on the skillet—wash it under very hot water, using a nonscratch nylon or chain mail scrubber—these are designed for cast iron, come clean in the dishwasher, and are guaranteed for a lifetime (see Sources, page 263). If there's still something left in the pan that's resisting scrubbing, use a little salt or baking soda and some paper towels. If the skillet loses its glow after a salt scrub, just reseason it.

If your skillet ever gets rusty, you can clean off the rust by scrubbing it with the flat side of a potato sliced in half plus some vegetable oil. Wipe out the rusty oil with paper towels, wash the pan well, and reseason.

RECLAIMING OLD SKILLETS

Yard sales are a great source of old skillets, which are real treasures. If a skillet you find hasn't been properly cared for, toss it into a campfire and let the burned-on bits burn off. Once it's cool, continue with a good scrub under hot water and then give it a good seasoning like the one I describe above. You can find all kinds of old cast-iron skillets—square ones, gigantic ones, deep ones. If you bring them back to life, they make great gifts—instant heirlooms.

eggs baked in tomatoes

The original version of this old country recipe didn't do much for me—it needed a lot more flavor. So I took it in an Italian direction, putting a little garlic butter under the eggs, along with some fresh basil, and topping the whole thing with Parmesan. Big difference! You can add a little chopped ham or even crumbled bacon with the garlic butter if you want it to be a bit more rib-sticking.

The juices the tomatoes give off in the cooking are really good, so be sure to serve them with grits or stacks of toast to soak them up. **SERVES 4**

1. Set the oven to 425 degrees.

2. Cut off the top third of each tomato and slice off a small piece of their bottoms so they can sit up straight, or the eggs may run out. Scoop out the insides with a spoon, leaving just the walls of the tomato shells (see Tip). Sprinkle well with salt and pepper inside and turn the shells upside down on a rack to drain while you make the garlic butter.

3. Mash the butter with a fork in a small bowl and work in the garlic bits evenly.

4. Arrange the drained tomato shells right side up in a shallow baking dish just large enough to hold them all. Drop a tablespoon of garlic butter into each tomato shell, followed by a torn-up basil leaf. Add the ham or bacon if you're using it.

5. Crack an egg into each tomato, sprinkle with salt and pepper, and scatter 1 tablespoon of the Parmesan evenly over each tomato. Try to leave a little yolk showing so you can tell how the egg is cooking later.

6. Slide the baking dish into the oven and bake until the egg whites are set but the yolks are still runny, close to 20 minutes. Garnish with slivers of basil if you like, and serve hot.

4 baseball-size ripe but firm tomatoes

Salt and ground black pepper

½ stick (4 tablespoons) butter, softened

1 garlic clove, pressed or minced

4 fresh basil leaves

¼ cup chopped ham or crumbled cooked bacon (optional)

4 large eggs in the shell, at room temperature

4 tablespoons shredded Parmesan cheese

Slivered fresh basil, for garnish

TIP

There's a lot of good tomato flavor in the scooped-out centers of the tomatoes. Save them to cook with okra or zucchini.

huffy-puffy oven pancake

This is a really unusual pancake that puffs up like magic, and you get a lot of oohs and aahs when you bring it to the table straight from the oven. The puff doesn't last long, so have everyone ready to raise their forks. You can serve it several ways: plain, with maple syrup and butter, or with some preserves and butter. But the most surprising, delicious way to serve it is with real cane syrup mixed with lemon juice and melted butter.

I used to think the cane syrup that comes in pretty bottles in the supermarket is the real thing, but it has just a tiny bit of actual cane syrup. Then I heard about someone who's brought back old-fashioned handmade cane syrup, and once I tasted his, I was amazed (see Sources, page 263). That real cane syrup is so good you won't believe the difference. Real cane syrup, fresh lemon juice, and melted butter take this pancake over the top.

The pancake will puff up even more if you make the batter the night before and refrigerate it until you're ready to bake it. **SERVES 4**

1. In a medium bowl with a pour spout, mix together the flour, milk, eggs, and nutmeg, mixing lightly and leaving the batter a bit lumpy. If you're making the batter the night before, cover the bowl with plastic wrap and refrigerate it overnight.

2. When you're ready to make the pancake, set the oven to 425 degrees.

3. Put the butter in a large ovenproof skillet or a large metal two-handled gratin dish about the same size, and slide the pan into the oven to melt the butter.

4. When the butter is hot and sizzling, pour the batter into the skillet or dish and bake until the pancake is all puffed up and golden brown in places, 15 to 20 minutes.

5. Meantime, if you're making the syrup: Mix together all the ingredients, pour into a small pitcher, and keep warm. As soon as the pancake comes out of the oven, dust it with confectioners' sugar, if you're using it. Cut the pancake in quarters and serve. Pass the syrup, if using.

½ cup all-purpose flour

½ cup milk

2 large eggs, lightly beaten with a fork

⅛ teaspoon grated nutmeg

½ stick (4 tablespoons) butter

Serving Syrup (optional)

¼ cup 100% real cane syrup (see Sources, page 263), warmed

Juice of ½ lemon

3 tablespoons butter, melted

Confectioners' sugar, for dusting the top of the pancake (optional)

fly-off-the-plate pancakes

I'm not sure why these pancakes are so good and so light—maybe it's the sour cream. You just have to make them for yourself and see what you think. The lightness means people can eat a lot of them and still want more, so be sure to have bacon or sausage or both on the side unless you want to make a second batch of pancakes—or just make a double batch and be done with it. SERVES 4

1. Resift the flour with the rest of the dry ingredients into a medium bowl.

2. Beat the egg, milk, and sour cream together in a medium bowl. Add the melted butter and stir it in with a whisk until smooth. Whisk the flour mixture into the egg mixture just until it all comes together.

3. Heat a griddle and when it's hot, drop a small spoonful of the batter onto it. If the batter seems too thick, add a little more milk, a tablespoon at a time, until it seems right when you test it.

4. You can make small or large pancakes, as you like. Flip them as usual—when the first side is getting bubbles at the edges—and then they're done in just another minute or two, when the other side is getting a little brown. Serve them straight from the griddle as you go, or keep warm on a plate in a 225-degree oven.

1 cup all-purpose flour, sifted

1 tablespoon sugar

1 tablespoon baking powder

¼ teaspoon salt

1 large egg, at room temperature

1 cup milk, plus more as needed

2 rounded tablespoons sour cream

2 tablespoons butter, melted and cooled

blackberry muffins

You can make these muffins with any berry, really—blueberries, raspberries, boysenberries, whatever tastes good. But my favorite is blackberries, especially those big juicy ones that sometimes come into the market in the winter from Central America, just when you're hoping for a promise of summer coming.

These aren't big old heavy muffins—they're light, and not overly sweet, with great flavor. MAKES 1 DOZEN MUFFINS

1. Set the oven to 400 degrees and adjust the rack position to the top third of the oven. Line a 12-cup muffin tin with cupcake liners or spray it with baking spray.

2. Sift the flour, sugar, cinnamon, and baking soda into a large bowl. Put the milk in a separate bowl and stir in the egg, melted butter, and lemon zest. Pour the wet ingredients onto the dry ingredients and very gently, using a fork, stir them just until the flour disappears. The muffins will be tough if you overmix the batter.

3. Stir in the berries so they're evenly distributed.

4. Fill the muffin cups three-quarters full and bake until golden brown on top, 20 to 25 minutes. Serve the muffins hot in a napkin-lined basket with plenty of butter to spread on them.

2 cups self-rising flour

¾ cup sugar

1½ teaspoons ground cinnamon

¼ teaspoon baking soda

1 cup milk

1 large egg, lightly beaten with a fork

1 stick (8 tablespoons) butter, melted and slightly cooled

1 teaspoon grated lemon zest

1 cup fresh blackberries

Butter, for serving

TIP

If you use very large blackberries, cut them in half. The juice will streak the muffins with a gorgeous color.

country fried apples

These spiced apple slices are great with sausage for breakfast, and they're also good with ham or roast pork for dinner. While they're cooking, they give off a wonderful apple pie aroma. The buttery spices are just irresistible. The number of servings you get depends on the size of the apples, whatever else you have on the table, and, of course, everyone's appetite.

It's best to cook these in a single layer in a skillet, so be sure to pull out your largest one. If you have too many apples for a single layer, putting the lid on the skillet will help the apples shrink down, but I think they taste best when they cook without a cover.

You can use butter or bacon drippings or a combination, as you like. I like all three versions, so it just depends what I have on hand. **SERVES 3 TO 6**

1. Cut the apples into quarters and cut out the cores, but don't peel them. Slice the quarters the long way so you get 3 or 4 thick slices out of each one.

2. Melt the butter (or bacon grease, or butter and grease) in a large skillet over medium heat. When it's bubbling, add the apple slices and turn them with a spatula to coat with the butter. If you cover them with a lid for a couple of minutes, they'll steam and cook a bit faster. Uncovered, they'll cook more slowly but they'll turn a lovely golden brown; that's how I do it.

3. Once the apples are soft, about 10 minutes, sprinkle the sugar over them, as little or as much as you'd like, and turn them again to be sure they have a little sugar on both sides. Sprinkle the spices on top and stir them up a bit. When the apples are smelling really good and looking almost caramelized, they're done. Give them a good squeeze or two of fresh lemon juice and serve hot.

3 crisp apples, such as Granny Smith

3 tablespoons butter or bacon grease, or a mixture of the two

About ¼ cup light brown sugar

A sprinkle each of ground cinnamon and grated nutmeg

A squeeze or two of fresh lemon juice

christmas morning cinnamon rolls
(or cinnamon bread or cinnamon raisin ring)

Aunt Laura got this recipe from a coworker at least sixty years ago, and she kind of forgot about it. But I love a good cinnamon roll, and I started fiddling with the recipe when Aunt Laura gave it to me. These rolls aren't like the ones you find at the airport that are just too much; they are smaller, lighter, and just a little sweet—though, of course, you can suit your own taste about how sweet you want them.

I know some people are scared to work with yeast, but really, it's not hard at all and it's a lot of fun to play with the dough and get it to feeling stretchy and plump and smooth, like a baby's bottom. That's when it's ready to form into the rolls. I promise you your family will be amazed by these yeasty rolls—and you can make all sorts of variations on the basic recipe, such as cinnamon bread or a cinnamon-raisin ring (see page 52) or Monkey Bread (page 91). They make a fine holiday breakfast treat. MAKES 24 ROLLS (OR 2 LOAVES OR ONE 9-INCH RING)

1. **To make the dough:** Sprinkle the yeast over the warm water in a small bowl, stir, and let sit for 5 minutes, or until the yeast is dissolved and creamy.

2. Drop the butter into the warm milk to melt it, then pour it all into a large bowl. Add the eggs, sugar, and salt and mix together well with a wooden spoon. Stir in the dissolved yeast. (This is the moment to stir in any add-ins, if you like.)

3. Add half the flour and beat with the spoon until smooth. Add the rest of the flour and beat again until the dough holds together; it will look shaggy. Turn the dough out onto a lightly floured surface, shape it into a ball, and let it rest for about 5 minutes.

4. Using floured hands, fold the dough in half, lifting the far edge of the ball and folding it toward you. (You don't actually knead this dough.) Pat it down some and then fold it in half

Dough

- 2 packets active dry yeast (4½ teaspoons)
- ¼ cup warm water
- 1 stick (8 tablespoons) butter, cut into 6 to 8 pieces
- 1 cup milk, warmed
- 3 large eggs, lightly beaten with a fork
- ½ cup sugar
- 2 teaspoons salt
- 5 cups all-purpose flour, plus more for shaping

Optional Add-Ins

- ½ cup chopped walnuts or pecans

or

- ¾ cup dried cranberries and 2 teaspoons grated orange zest

continued...

again and once again; it will start to feel smooth and stretchy. (You can make the dough ahead, wrap it well, and freeze it for up to 4 weeks until you're ready to defrost it and proceed.)

5. To make cinnamon rolls: Set the oven to 425 degrees. Line two 8-inch round cake pans with parchment paper (press the paper over the bottom of the upside-down pan to make an outline and cut the circle out).

6. Mix the sugars and cinnamon together.

7. Pat the dough out into a skinny rope shape about 30 inches long, smoothing it gently with your fingers. Cut the loaf crosswise in half and, working quickly, so the dough doesn't get too soft and loose, cut each half into 12 equal slices, about 1¼ inches thick, to make 24 pieces.

8. To shape the rolls: One by one, take each slice and pat and pull it out until it's about 8 inches long. Sprinkle 1½ teaspoons of the cinnamon-sugar mixture for the topping along the strip. Starting at one end, roll the strip of dough into a tight little rosebud shape, winding the length of it tightly around the center. Arrange 12 rolls evenly in each pan, setting them in a ring around the edges of the pan with the spiral facing up and butting them up against each other so they'll hold their shape when they bake; leave the center of the pan empty so they can expand.

9. Brush the rolls all over with melted butter and sprinkle each one with ½ teaspoon of the cinnamon sugar—you'll have a little left over. Drizzle with the remaining melted butter.

10. Bake until the rolls are lightly brown and springy, bouncing back when you pat their tops, about 15 minutes. Serve hot with butter.

continued...

or

¾ cup dried blueberries and 1 tablespoon grated lemon zest

Topping (for Cinnamon Rolls and Cinnamon Bread)

½ cup white sugar

½ cup dark brown sugar

2 tablespoons ground cinnamon

½ stick (4 tablespoons) butter, melted

Filling (for Cinnamon Raisin Ring)

¼ cup dark brown sugar

1 teaspoon ground cinnamon

½ stick (4 tablespoons) butter, softened

⅓ cup raisins

Melted butter, for brushing

Butter, for serving

> **TIP**
>
> One nice thing about this dough (which also works for Monkey Bread, page 91) is that you can freeze it all kinds of ways: as dough or as rolls right in the baking pan (bake them after returning them to room temperature), or as baked rolls or bread. All will keep in the freezer, well wrapped, for up to 4 weeks.

11. To make cinnamon bread: Set the oven to 425 degrees. Line a baking sheet with parchment paper.

12. Mix the sugar and cinnamon together.

13. Cut the dough in half and put the halves on the baking sheet. Pat each piece into a long ropy shape about 15 inches long, smoothing it with your fingers. Brush all over with melted butter, then sprinkle the cinnamon sugar thickly and evenly on top. Using a sharp knife, make 6 even diagonal slashes in the top of each loaf.

14. Bake until the bread is lightly browned and springy to the touch, about 22 minutes. Serve hot with butter.

15. To make the cinnamon-raisin ring: Set the oven to 425 degrees. Line a 9-inch cake pan with parchment paper.

16. Roll the dough out on a floured surface into a rectangle about 8 inches by 12 inches.

17. Mix the sugar with the cinnamon. Smear the soft butter all over the dough rectangle and sprinkle the cinnamon sugar evenly over the top. Scatter over the raisins and press them in lightly.

18. Starting at a long side, roll the dough up tightly into a roll about 26 inches long, using your palms to extend it. Carefully arrange the roll seam side down up against the sides of the pan, pinching the ends together as seamlessly as you can. Using kitchen scissors, cut deep diagonal slashes into the dough roll about every 1½ inches. Brush the ring with melted butter.

19. Bake until the ring is lightly browned and springs back when touched, about 25 minutes. To serve, cut through the slashes to make individual slices and serve warm with butter.

20. The rolls or bread will keep for at least 4 days at room temperature, well wrapped.

scrumptious bacon

Everybody loves this little-bit-sweet, little-bit-spicy bacon so much that it's hard to stop making it once you know about it. Sometimes I've gotten too busy and over-cooked it, but people still insist on eating it, it's that good. Don't worry that it's going to be too spicy. The cayenne just gives it a little afterglow.

It's essential to have thick-sliced bacon, and the better the bacon you start with, the better it will end up. You can make it ahead and it will keep for a couple of days in a tightly sealed tin in a cool spot. But if anyone knows it's there, it won't be there long. **SERVES 4 TO 6**

1. Set the oven to 350 degrees. Line a baking sheet with foil and put a rack on top, so the fat can drain off as the bacon cooks. Separate the bacon into slices.

2. Mix the sugar, cayenne, and black pepper on a plate and spread out the mixture. Press one side of each bacon slice onto the spicy sugar and arrange them sugar side up on the rack on the baking sheet.

3. Bake until the bacon is golden brown, about 35 minutes—but start checking at 25 minutes. Remove the entire rack of bacon to a paper towel–lined platter to drain.

4. When the bacon is cool, break each slice into 2 or 3 pieces. Serve, or store in a tightly sealed tin in a cool spot for up to 2 days.

1 pound thick-sliced bacon

⅓ cup light brown sugar

½ teaspoon cayenne

Freshly ground black pepper to taste

TIP

You can serve the bacon pieces with drinks or break them up over salads or side dishes. And this bacon makes awesome BLTs.

TIP

I should confess that sometimes I double up on the seasoned sugar and do both sides. Is that twice as good? You'll have to try it for yourself.

some things you have to know how to make to be a good southern cook

GREAT FRIED CHICKEN makes its home in the South. If you're going to be a good Southern cook, you'd better bone up on your fried chicken. And your cornbread, your dirty rice, and your country collard greens. Where I live, in the Georgia Lowcountry by the coast, you also have to cook great shrimp and grits, and since the whole world has fallen in love with that dish, you'd better brush up on that one too. And if you can't make a really good biscuit, you're in trouble down here.

These powerful dishes are at the heart of our country Southern food, the timeless dishes that define us. They're the ones we crave when we're away from them, and we know we're home when they're on the table again. Although you can still get this kind of homey food in a few restaurants in the South, mostly it's home-cooked food, and I always think it tastes best when someone who loves you makes it for you.

Back in the slave days—which were not so very long ago—there were grand versions of the same kinds of dishes served in the Plantation House, made with exotic spices and the best ingredients to be found. They were cooked by "Old Hands" like my great-grandmother, who earned the status of a house slave because of her skills in the kitchen. But she also knew how to season plainer foods and scraps, how to get the most flavor out of every little bit.

I'm proud to have a place in this long line of good cooks. Both my Grandmother Hattie and I started to learn how to cook when we were six years old, and our teachers cut us no slack. We had to get it right, doing it over and over and over until it was in our bones. In the South, we call that know-it-in-your-bones, no-recipe kind of cooking "cooking by ear." In fact, I hadn't written down most of these recipes before. But here they are now, and you can make your family and friends at the Southern table as glad as mine are.

I think one reason Southerners are usually such good cooks is that they learn early to cook foods that inspire fear in novice cooks elsewhere: fried chicken and fried green tomatoes, biscuits, okra, grits, gravy... it's a long list. But fear not, the secrets are all here for foolproof Southern food.

panfried chicken

If any one dish says Southern cooking, it's fried chicken. Popeye's is good, but great fried chicken is what you get at home. How do I make mine so good? I take my time with it, starting the day before with a buttermilk soak combined with some great seasoning. I massage the spices into the chicken thoroughly and carefully but gently, covering every bit of it. If you can't remember to do it ahead, you can do a quick buttermilk soak the morning of the day you want to serve it, but then you should up the seasoning a little. Making fried chicken is an act of love, and you want to put your full attention into it.

You can cut a frying chicken into serving pieces, so everyone can have their choice of white or dark meat. Or, if you know everyone is going to want dark meat, buy a package of chicken thighs or drumsticks. For frying, choose your pan carefully. As with so many other things I cook, I like to use my grandmother's well-seasoned cast-iron skillet with a glass lid. If you're not lucky enough to have one of those, just use a deep heavy skillet—a Le Creuset–type iron skillet with an enamel coating works very well. You can also use a Dutch oven. The important thing is that you don't fill the skillet too full with fat, or you risk it boiling over when you add the chicken. If your skillet has a little spout (for pouring off the grease), this works like a vent when the pan is covered, so you can use more fat.

I like to use Crisco for frying chicken because it gives it a very crisp coating and a succulent taste. You can use peanut oil, lard, or a mixture, as you like. All of them will contribute fine flavor. A deep-fat thermometer should register 375 degrees— that's the right frying temperature. The temperature will drop when you add the chicken, so make sure it returns to 375 degrees once the pieces are all in the skillet.

SERVES 4

1. Rinse the chicken well and leave it wet so the seasoning will stick to it. In a big bowl, sprinkle the Savannah seasoning over the chicken pieces and massage it in gently, using your hands. Pour on just enough buttermilk to coat the chicken well—you don't want any buttermilk in a puddle in the bottom of the bowl. Using your hands, turn the chicken pieces in the buttermilk so that every piece is well covered. Cover the bowl with plastic wrap and refrigerate overnight.

2. Take the chicken out of the refrigerator when you're ready to fry it.

3. Put the flour in a clean paper bag and shake it up. Put the Crisco, oil, lard, or bacon grease in a large deep skillet or a Dutch oven—remember not to fill it more than halfway with fat—and set it over medium heat.

4. While the fat is heating, lift one piece of chicken at a time out of the bowl, shake it off, and drop it into the bag with the flour. Close the top of the bag and shake. Check to be sure the chicken is well covered with flour all over, then put it on a large plate. When you have enough pieces floured to just fill your skillet (you want to fry in batches so you don't crowd the chicken pieces), check that the oil is hot enough: 375 degrees on a deep-fat thermometer. Or, if you don't have a thermometer, flick a little flour into the hot fat; if it sizzles, you're ready to fry. Starting with the dark pieces, carefully add the chicken to the hot oil, one piece at a time, skin side down. The oil should keep bubbling and the thermometer should stay at around 375 degrees. When the skillet is full, cover with a lid—a glass lid is best, so you can watch carefully to be sure the oil is bubbling gently and isn't about to boil over and so you can see how the chicken is browning.

5. Fry the chicken, turning each piece with tongs, until it's well browned on both sides—you don't want it too light—about 7 minutes per side for white meat and 9 minutes per side for dark meat. Any really large pieces will take a few minutes longer at least. (If you're deep-frying in a Dutch oven, it'll go faster; cook the chicken about 10 minutes altogether, turning it frequently so it browns evenly.) You can test a thigh or a drumstick with the point of a knife to make sure the juices run clear. If you have an instant-read thermometer, the temperature

1 frying chicken (about 4 pounds), cut up, or 4 pounds thighs or drumsticks (be sure the pieces are small), any loose skin removed

1 tablespoon plus 2 teaspoons Dora's Savannah Seasoning (page 79)

1 quart buttermilk, or as needed

About 1 cup self-rising flour

About 1½ pounds (6 cups) Crisco, or 6 cups peanut oil, lard, or bacon grease

TIPS

• If you haven't made fried chicken before, see Talking About Frying (page 144).

• Self-rising flour is the key to a crunchy crust—don't substitute regular flour. If you don't have self-rising flour, make some; see page 75.

should read 165 degrees. If the meatiest part is not cooked through but the chicken is well browned, remove it to a rack set over a baking sheet, put it in a 325-degree oven, and test again in 5 minutes.

6. As soon as the chicken is done, remove it to paper towels to drain briefly. Between batches, scoop out any coating that's fallen off the chicken into the oil with a slotted spoon so it doesn't burn and ruin the taste of the frying fat.

7. Serve the chicken hot or at room temperature. Leftover chicken is just wonderful, of course.

> **TIPS**
>
> • Instead of using paper towels, you can drain the fried chicken on a rack set over a cookie sheet. If you fold some brown paper grocery bags and place them under the rack, you can just toss them out later and be done with any mess.
>
> • The fried-chicken grease left in the pan is wonderful for flavoring greens or fried cornbread. Let it cool, then pour it into a jar, cover, and keep it in the refrigerator. Label and date it to avoid any mysteries later. In my house, I use the fried-chicken grease so often that I don't need to date it or refrigerate it; I keep the jar by the stove.
>
> • If the chicken pieces are large, turn the heat down a bit and cook them longer. Otherwise, they will get too brown or the chicken will be red at the bone even if it's golden brown on the outside. Or finish them in the oven once they're browned.
>
> • Leftover fried chicken can be reheated in the oven at 200 degrees for 15 minutes.

smothered chicken

Smothering is what you do to leftover fried chicken—or ribs or pork chops—and some people like it even better than the original dish. You need leftover pan gravy or some chicken-frying grease. That will be your base for the smothering gravy. Add a little flour while you're heating it up and stir it in well, so there are no lumps. Cook it over medium heat until it's thickened and the flour has cooked a bit, then taste it to make sure it's right. Add the meat to the pan, cover, and cook for 20 minutes over medium-low heat.

Serve over warm grits, mashed potatoes, or rice.

buttermilk cornbread

It's always time for cornbread—breakfast, lunch, dinner, or snack time. My grandfather would break his leftover cornbread up into a bowl and pour on some buttermilk. My brother will eat cornbread straight from the refrigerator. Cornbread is perfect with vegetables or even just heated up and served with the warmed leftover potlikker from vegetables. Cornbread and gravy. Cornbread with cane syrup poured on top is always a hit. If my family has a sacred dish, it's my grandmother's cornbread dressing (page 198), which is always on the table during the holiday season. Down here, cornbread could hardly be more important or beloved.

My cornbread is my grandmother's, and I cook it in my favorite kitchen utensil, her well-seasoned cast-iron skillet. It's not a yellow-cornmeal cornbread—I always use white cornmeal, because it tastes much more delicate to me and I don't like the mealy texture of yellow cornmeal very much. There are a couple of other unusual things about this cornbread. I put just a little sugar in the batter, and when the cornbread is just out of the oven, I rub it all over the top with the end of a stick of butter so it glistens. Once the butter is melted in, serve it right away with more butter—use that same stick—on the side. **SERVES 6**

1. Set the oven to 350 degrees. Adjust the racks to the upper and lower positions of the oven.

2. Cook the bacon in an 8-inch cast-iron skillet over medium-high heat until it is crisp and the fat is rendered. Set the bacon aside and pour the grease into a Pyrex measuring cup. You'll need about ⅓ cup grease; if you don't have enough, cook up some more bacon. You can crumble the cooked bacon and add it to the cornbread batter before it goes into the skillet if you like, or save it for another meal. Put the skillet in the oven.

3. In a medium bowl, stir together the cornmeal, flour, and sugar with a wooden spoon. Add the buttermilk and water and mix well. Crack the eggs into the bowl, and mix well (see Tip).

4. When the skillet is hot, add 2 tablespoons of the bacon grease and roll it around to cover the bottom and sides. Mix the remaining bacon grease into the cornbread batter. Add the crumbled bacon if you're using it. Pour the batter into the hot

4 fatty bacon slices (or more if your bacon is lean)

2 cups white cornmeal

1 cup self-rising flour

2 tablespoons sugar

1 cup buttermilk

1 cup water

2 large eggs

1 stick (8 tablespoons) butter, for glazing and serving, or 1 large pat (about 2 tablespoons) butter, for glazing

skillet and place on the bottom rack of the oven to bake until set, about 20 minutes.

5. When it's set, move the cornbread to the top rack to brown. When it's done, the top will be lightly browned with cracks— this will take just a few minutes, so watch it carefully.

6. Remove the cornbread from the oven and rub the top generously all over with the end of the stick of butter or with the pat of butter stuck on the tines of a fork. When the butter is melted, slice the cornbread in the skillet and serve right away, with more butter on the side if you like.

TIP

Any time you need to mix an egg or two into a batter, you can break up the yolks right in the bowl using the edge of a wooden spoon, cutting up and down several times for each yolk.

fry-meat grease

I always say you should save the cooking grease in which you've fried something delicious, like chicken or pork chops or sausage patties—and, of course, the grease that renders out when you fry bacon. In the South, we call all this fry-meat grease, and it's packed with flavor, ready to season your greens or your rice or anything you think might be improved by it. You can give almost anything savory a huge boost by using just a little of this highly seasoned fat instead of starting it off with a flavorless oil.

I always rub my sweet potatoes all over with fry-meat grease before I bake them, just like my grandmother did—even if I'm going to peel them afterward. That wonderful taste goes right through the skin into the potatoes while they're in the hot oven.

Saving fry-meat grease is thrifty too; it's just crazy to throw it out, which is what most people do. Instead, be smart: When it's cool, pour the grease into a jar with a tight lid, label and date the jar, and store it in the refrigerator for up to 10 days (longer for bacon grease). It's money in the flavor bank.

My grandmother had a stainless steel grease container with a strainer on top to filter out big crumbs. I have one that holds 6 cups and has a good filter (see Sources, page 263).

next-day fried greens and rice

I know quite a few people who won't eat collard greens for dinner but want me to make a lot of them so they can have leftovers fried with rice for lunch the next day. I can't really disagree with that idea, although I love them the first time too. They really *are* better the next day. You stir and fry them in a skillet with some rice (also left over) and butter—a bit more greens than rice. Some meat should go in too, either left from cooking the collards or freshly cooked bacon.

Finish off the dish with some hot sauce, pepper, and vinegar and serve it with cornbread—that's one of the best meals you'll ever eat. And it doesn't even have a real name.

pepper vinegar

A plate of collards isn't complete without a splash or two of pepper vinegar, and most Southern tables will have a bottle right there next to the salt and pepper. You can make your own pepper vinegar in the fall when the little hot peppers come into the market, and it will be ready to give as Christmas presents. You need bottles with small necks, like sauce bottles. Run them through the dishwasher, and the caps too. Fill the bottles with well-rinsed stemmed skinny little peppers— red, yellow, orange, green, any color. Bring some distilled white vinegar—adding salt if you like, about 1 teaspoon salt to 4 cups vinegar—to a boil and pour it over the peppers to fill the bottles. Let them cool uncapped. Top off the bottles with more vinegar as needed and cover them with the clean caps. Let them season for 6 weeks, then keep a bottle on the table to sprinkle over greens.

dirty brown rice

Dirty rice has always been a favorite at our family table, but one day I had the idea to play around with it a little, to make it a little healthier and give it a good chewy texture. So I left out the meat, used brown rice instead of white, and added some fresh vegetables. Although it's a lot lighter than the original, it's very satisfying, because it tastes so good and has that chewiness that makes you feel like you've eaten something that will keep you going for a long time.

You can cook the brown rice way ahead of time, even the day before, and if you do that, you can whip this dish up in no time. (You can also use the Foolproof Rice recipe on page 220, which uses white rice.) I like to make a double batch of plain rice so I'll have leftovers to play with another day. **SERVES 4 TO 6**

1. To cook the rice: Bring the water to a boil in a 2-quart covered saucepan. When it boils, add the salt and stir in the rice. Cover and cook over medium-high heat until the rice is tender-chewy, about 45 minutes. (You should have about 3 cups cooked rice.) Leave it off the heat on the stovetop, covered, for a while, while you start making the dirty rice. Or, if you're making the dirty rice the next day, let the rice cool and then refrigerate it in a covered container.

2. To dirty the rice: Heat a large skillet over medium heat and melt the butter in it. Add the mushrooms, green pepper, onions, and garlic and season with a little salt and pepper. Stir well, turn the heat up to medium-high, and cook until the onions are translucent, about 5 minutes.

3. Add the cooked rice cup by cup, stirring as you go. Turn the heat down to medium-low and add the parsley and a little bit more salt and pepper. Stir well and continue cooking until the rice is hot. Serve right away. Or steam it in a microwave oven sprinkled with water if it seems dry.

Brown Rice

2½ cups water
¼ teaspoon salt
1 cup brown rice

The Dirtying

5 tablespoons butter
2 cups chopped white mushrooms (about ½ pound)
1 cup chopped green bell pepper
1 cup chopped yellow onion
1 tablespoon pressed or minced garlic
Salt and ground black pepper to taste
2–3 tablespoons dried parsley (to make the rice a little dirtier)

> **TIP**
> Leftovers are just fine the next day. Reheat the rice by steaming it in a covered pot over low heat.

shrimp and grits

This is one of those great dishes that can make you weep with pleasure. In the old days in the Lowcountry, it was a breakfast dish, but it's become so popular that we eat it for dinner now. You can even serve my version to company, because it's a little bit elegant with the Boursin cheese and white wine. It's also very rich, so serve it with a sharp lemony green salad. SERVES 4 TO 6

1. In a large nonstick skillet, heat the olive oil over medium-high heat and cook the bacon until golden. Remove the bacon with a slotted spoon and drain on paper towels.

2. Pour out all but 2 tablespoons of the fat from the skillet. Stir in the cream, Boursin, wine, chives, salt, and pepper and stir constantly over medium heat to make a slightly thickened sauce, a few minutes. Once the sauce is smooth, add the shrimp and cook until they're pink all over and cooked through, about 5 minutes.

3. Spoon a serving of warm grits onto each plate and top with the shrimp in their sauce. Divide the bacon bits among the plates and serve immediately.

1 tablespoon extra-virgin olive oil

3 bacon slices, stacked up and sliced thin crosswise

1½ cups heavy cream

2 tablespoons shallot-and-chive Boursin cheese

2 tablespoons dry white wine

2 tablespoons snipped fresh chives

1 teaspoon salt

¼ teaspoon ground black pepper

1 pound large (21–25 count) shrimp, peeled and deveined

Down-Home Country Grits (page 36), kept warm

mayonnaise biscuits

These are the biscuits to make if you think you can't make biscuits. That was once me, and this is the recipe that turned me into a biscuit baker. It was my good friend Jellyroll who came up with the magic recipe and taught it to me, and I bless her every time I make these. They're drop biscuits: If you use an ice cream scoop, they're all the same size and you look like a pro. **MAKES 12 BISCUITS**

1. Set the oven to 350 degrees. Spray a baking sheet with baking spray.

2. Dump the flour and mayonnaise into a large bowl, then add the milk slowly, mixing it in with a wooden spoon. The dough needs to be loose enough to drop easily from the ice cream scoop—if it's not, add more milk, a tiny bit at a time, and mix it in until the dough will drop from the scoop. Flour your hands and knead the dough right in the bowl until it just holds together, less than 10 turns.

3. Flour an ice cream scoop or a ¼-cup measuring cup, fill with dough, and drop the dough onto the baking sheet. Continue making biscuits, spacing them so that they're right next to each other. Flour the scoop again as needed.

4. Bake the biscuits until golden brown, 15 to 20 minutes. Serve hot with plenty of butter.

3 cups self-rising flour

1 cup mayonnaise

¾ cup milk, or more if needed
   Butter, for serving

TIP
You can also pat the dough out 1 inch thick on a floured board and cut it into square biscuits.

talking about flours

Part of the reason Southerners make such wonderful biscuits, quick breads, cakes, and pies is that our flour is different. It's made from red winter wheat, which is softer, has less protein, and is more finely milled than flour everywhere else in the country, and that makes our baked goods lighter and more tender. White Lily used to be the flour most Southerners wanted in their kitchens, but since it started being produced in the Midwest, Southern bakers swear it's not the same. I've always liked Martha White flour, and that's the one I still use for biscuits—the self-rising version, which has baking powder and salt added to it.

NORTHERN ALL-PURPOSE FLOUR is more like bread flour, which is 12 to 14 percent protein, because Yankees make a lot more yeast bread than we do. Cake flour is closer to Southern flour, only 6 to 8 percent protein. All-purpose flour is in the middle, 10 to 12 percent protein.

I use self-rising MARTHA WHITE for dredging fried food too, because the baking powder in it makes the fried food crisper. You can make your own self-rising flour by adding 1½ teaspoons baking powder and ½ teaspoon salt to a cupful of all-purpose flour, but it won't be as finely milled as the Southern flour. Commercial self-rising flour has the baking powder and salt mixed in very thoroughly, so there's no chance you'll get a little bitter taste of baking powder—try to do the same. A flour sifter does a good job.

You can mail-order Martha White flour if you're homesick (see Sources, page 263). King Arthur also makes a good self-rising flour that's widely distributed and can be mail-ordered too. Just remember that baking powder isn't forever—6 months, and it's on its way out. So it's a good idea to date your self-rising flour if you don't use it often and toss it after 6 months.

It's smart to keep flour in the freezer, tightly wrapped. That way you don't have to worry about humidity affecting the flour—and your results. The flour will keep fresh longer too.

Save cake flour for cakes—I tell you in each recipe which flour will work best.

sprightly biscuits

These biscuits are buttery, feathery, and so fragrant while they're baking that people can't wait for them to come out of the oven. It's the Sprite (or 7-Up) that makes them light. Once you've nailed this recipe and everyone is begging you to make them again and again, try the Mayonnaise Biscuits (page 74) and Cream Biscuits (page 233) too. I promise they'll work just as perfectly. Each of them has a secret ingredient that makes all the difference. **MAKES 9 BISCUITS**

1. Set the oven to 425 degrees.

2. In a large bowl, mix the Bisquick, buttermilk, Sprite or 7-Up, and sugar with a wooden spoon. Gather the dough together into a ball and gently pat or roll it out 1 inch thick on a floured surface (or just use more Bisquick on the rolling surface).

3. Put the butter in a 9-inch round cake pan and set it in the oven to melt.

4. Meanwhile, using a biscuit cutter or the rim of a 3-inch-wide drinking glass, cut out biscuits, without twisting the cutter. (If you twist, they won't rise as high.)

5. When the butter's melted, remove the pan from the oven and, using a large spatula to lift the biscuits, arrange them around the edge of the pan, setting them into the melted butter, placing one in the center. Bake the biscuits until golden on top, 8 to 10 minutes. The tops should spring back when touched.

6. Cover the pan with a plate, flip the biscuits over onto it, and serve immediately, with more butter on the side and, if you like, cane syrup or molasses to drizzle over the top.

2 cups Bisquick
½ cup buttermilk
½ cup Sprite or 7-Up
2 tablespoons sugar
1 stick (8 tablespoons) butter
Butter, for serving
Cane syrup or molasses, for topping (optional)

TIP

The recipe doubles perfectly, for 18 biscuits. Just use two cake pans and melt a stick of butter in each one, and double the other ingredients.

fried green tomatoes

In my part of the country, there are always green tomatoes available. In other areas you may have to ask, but usually there's a box of very green tomatoes way in the back somewhere in the market. Look for ones with no red shoulders.

This recipe comes from my Aunt Laura, and it makes crisp fried green tomatoes with a little kick. Serve them hot from the skillet, while they're still perfectly crisp. If you fry them in bacon grease or fried-chicken grease, they'll be especially delicious. Try them for breakfast with fried eggs and sausage. SERVES 4

1. Have ready a baking rack set over a baking sheet for draining the fried tomatoes.

2. Salt and pepper the tomato slices. Mix together the flour, cornmeal, and seasoning in a shallow bowl.

3. Beat the buttermilk and egg together in a shallow bowl with a fork. If the egg and buttermilk mixture seems too thick for dipping the tomato slices, add a little water to thin it.

4. Heat a heavy skillet over medium heat and when it's hot, add the frying oil, or melt the butter. When the oil is hot, dip a tomato slice in the flour mixture, then in the buttermilk and egg, and then in the flour again, shaking off any excess. Slide the tomato slice into the skillet and repeat until the skillet is full. Turn the slices when they're golden brown on the first side, about 2 minutes, and cook on the second side until golden brown. Remove the tomato slices to the rack to drain. Repeat with the remaining tomato slices. Serve immediately.

Salt and ground black pepper to taste

3 fat green tomatoes, cut into ½-inch-thick slices

1 cup self-rising flour

½ cup cornmeal

1½ teaspoons Dora's Savannah Seasoning (page 79)

¼ cup buttermilk

1 large egg

¼ cup frying oil, such as bacon grease or fried-chicken grease, or ½ stick (4 tablespoons) butter

TIP

You may have to wipe out the pan if the flour starts to burn on the bottom. Start again with fresh oil if that happens.

my savannah seasoning

I keep this basic spicy seasoning mix in a little jar by the stovetop, I use it that often. It's good with almost everything from eggs to chicken to pork and even some vegetables, and you can save yourself a little time making it up ahead.

Always taste what you're cooking once it's gone in, because you may find you need a little more of one or two elements to bring up the flavor.   MAKES ABOUT ⅔ CUP

⅓ cup Lawry's Seasoned Salt
¼ cup salt
2 scant tablespoons granulated garlic or garlic powder
1 tablespoon freshly ground black pepper

In a small bowl, mix everything together very thoroughly. Store the seasoning in a tightly sealed glass jar. It will keep for up to 3 months.

quick, some bread for the table!

ONE THING THAT MAKES A HOME-COOKED MEAL in the South such a pleasure is the basket of hot homemade biscuits, rolls, or muffins that's usually served with it. Or it can be a skillet full of cornbread right out of the oven. Or hot hoecakes, which we call fried cornbread. There might be several kinds of bread in the basket, including banana bread. That basket, with its fresh napkin keeping these little breads warm, says you're welcome at this table and that someone cared enough about everyone there to make something special. Other things on the table speak this way too—the pepper vinegar and other condiments and pickles people love to see there.

It takes very little time to make these special little Southern touches, and I urge you to try to make it a habit. These breads take less than five minutes' work and about twenty minutes in the oven while you do something else.

There are other great quick breads hidden all over the book too—Buttermilk Cornbread (page 64), Sprightly Biscuits (page 77), Mayonnaise Biscuits (page 74), and Cream Biscuits (page 233) are all part of this fine tradition.

OPPOSITE: Dora and her aunt Laura Daniels

hoecakes (fried cornbread)

My grandmother used to make these little cornbread cakes for us, and I love to make them for my grandchildren too. People outside Savannah know them as hoe-cakes, but we just call them fried cornbread. Whatever name you use, you can't go wrong with them—everyone loves them, and they're so easy. They're great as pancakes for breakfast with a little cane syrup drizzled over them, or alongside a mess of greens, or as an alternative to cornbread or biscuits with lunch or dinner. They have a nice crisp crust on the outside and a soft, sweet corn flavor inside.

I like white cornmeal better than yellow for grits or cornbread, and for just about anything. To me, yellow cornmeal and yellow grits have a texture that's a little too grainy. The yellow also takes longer to cook—a lot of people don't know that.

If you saved the flavorful frying grease from making fried chicken, you'll be glad you did when you add a spoonful to this batter.

This recipe makes a small batch. Double or triple it if you need to feed a big family or a lot of friends. The batter will keep for a couple of days in the refrigerator. **SERVES 4**

1. In a bowl, mix together the dry ingredients with a wooden spoon. Add the buttermilk slowly. Mix in the egg, cutting into the yolk with the spoon's edge to help it mix in better. Add the water and fat or oil and stir well. The texture should be like thick soup, so you may need to add more water.

2. I like to fry the cornbread cakes in my grandmother's cast-iron skillet or on a flat iron griddle, but any skillet or griddle will be fine. Heat the skillet or griddle over medium heat and grease it well with the fat of your choice (butter is delicious, but it tends to burn unless you mix it with a little oil). Once the skillet is hot and the fat is sizzling, drop the batter from a ⅛-cup (2-tablespoon) measure into the skillet, in batches if necessary. Fry the cakes until the edges are bubbling and the centers are set, then flip with a spatula to fry them on the other side until they're done. Like with pancakes, you can't say how long it will take, but the second side always cooks faster than the first. If the cakes seem greasy, drain them on paper towels before serving hot.

½ cup self-rising white cornmeal (see Sources, page 263)

½ cup self-rising flour

2 teaspoons sugar

⅓ cup buttermilk

1 large egg

⅓ cup water, or more as needed

2 tablespoons melted fat or oil: bacon grease, fried-chicken grease, butter, or vegetable oil

Butter or mixed butter and vegetable oil, for frying

TIP

If you're fresh out of self-rising cornmeal and/or flour, add 1½ teaspoons baking powder and ½ teaspoon salt to each cup of cornmeal or flour.

TIPS

• If you don't have a fryer basket, use a slotted spoon to nudge the pups as they fry to roll them over and then to lift them out when they're done.

• You can filter the cooled oil through a coffee filter and store it, covered, in the refrigerator for up to 1 month. You can reuse it up to two more times, as long as it smells fresh.

hushpuppies

Does anyone *not* love hushpuppies? Everyone I know is crazy for these deep-fried cornmeal cakes, and I am too. I like them very crunchy on the outside and light on the inside. Sometimes they can be real sinkers. Not these. They have beer in them, which makes them lighter. Use an electric fryer with a basket or a Dutch oven with a fry basket to make them (see Tips).

Some people dip their hushpuppies into all sorts of things, like tartar sauce and soft butter, but I don't. **SERVES 6**

1. Mix all the dry ingredients in a medium bowl. In another bowl, beat the eggs with a fork, then add the sour cream, beer, onion, garlic, and parsley and mix together. Add the dry ingredients to the wet ingredients and mix everything together well with a rubber spatula. Don't overmix, which would toughen the hushpuppies. The batter will be thick. Let it sit, covered, in the fridge for 30 minutes.

2. Shortly before you're ready to fry, pour the oil into a deep fryer or Dutch oven to a depth of at least 3 inches. Heat to 375 degrees on a deep-fry thermometer. To form the puppies, you can use a ½-tablespoon measure (the size I like), or a small ice cream scoop (1½ tablespoons). Have ready a cup of water to clean off any leftover batter from the spoon or scoop before the next pup goes in, as well as a bowl lined with paper towels.

3. When the oil is ready, drop in the fry basket and, one by one, drop the puppies into the basket, cleaning the spoon or scoop in the water as you go. The pups will usually turn themselves right over to cook their other side. If they don't, shake the basket to encourage them. When they're nice and crisp on the outside and a deep golden brown, 3 to 4 minutes, pull out the basket and drain the pups in the paper towel–lined bowl and start the next batch. Serve as fast as you can.

1½ cups stone-ground white cornmeal

½ cup self-rising flour

2 tablespoons sugar

½ teaspoon baking powder

½ teaspoon salt

2 large eggs

½ cup sour cream

½ cup beer (not dark)

Generous ½ cup finely chopped onion

1 large garlic clove, pressed or minced

1 tablespoon chopped fresh parsley

Vegetable oil or lard, for frying

TIP

If you can't find stone-ground white cornmeal, just use whatever you can find—white or yellow, self-rising or not. They all work just fine, but if you use self-rising cornmeal, skip the baking powder and the salt.

why do i...

USE SELF-RISING FLOUR?

Lots of Southern cooks keep this on hand because it contains the right amounts of baking powder and salt for making biscuits and other everyday foods. It saves time, and the flour is also made from soft Southern wheat, which gives you more tender baked goods. If you're using it for dusting something before frying it, it clings well and the baking powder helps to make a crisp crust on the food.

USE WHITE CORNMEAL & WHITE GRITS?

I prefer the flavor, which I think is more delicate. Dried yellow corn always seems too corny and mealy for me, and it's just a little bit sweeter and takes a little longer to cook. You might like yellow better (Yankees do), which is fine by me.

USE CERTAIN CONVENIENCE FOODS?

Sometimes it's because these are actually convenient, but I usually don't use them to save time. You may notice that I make them *inconvenient*, for instance, by cooking quick-cooking grits for over an hour. It's almost always flavor that I'm looking for, either good flavor on its own or flavor I can make even more delicious by adding my own touches to it. I can't improve on Lawry's Seasoned Salt, so I use it often, but always with other spices too; it just gives me a head start.

CHOOSE THE FATTEST BACON AT THE GROCERY STORE?

Everyone else is usually looking for lean, but to me, the fat is the best part. I'll cook up most of a pound of bacon just to get a good amount of bacon grease for flavoring my dishes. That's like liquid gold in the flavor bank. Even if I'm just serving bacon on its own, for breakfast or for a sandwich, I cook it crisp so most of the fat goes into my bacon grease jar, and the crisp fat is especially delicious. Limp bacon with fat that isn't cooked long enough just doesn't appeal to me.

RINSE RAW CHICKEN BEFORE I COOK IT?

I know, I know, the experts say not to do that, but I don't do it to only clean the chicken. I do it also so the seasoning will stick to the chicken and flavor it, usually overnight, before I cook it the next day. It does make a difference. And the chicken is cooked long enough that you don't have to worry about bacteria getting spread around from the rinsing.

NOT SAY WHETHER TO USE SALTED OR UNSALTED BUTTER?

I think it's a matter of personal taste. If you want or need to limit your salt, you'll use unsalted. And remember, if you're using self-rising flour, the salt is already added for you.

I always used to use margarine, which I thought was healthier (and cheaper), though a number of my old family recipes called for "pure butter." Now we know margarine isn't the healthiest choice. I love to use butter, especially the Irish butter called Kerrygold, which comes from grass-fed cows. It's expensive, but you can buy it at warehouse clubs for less. Kerrygold salted is quite salty, so if salt is a concern for you, use unsalted.

garlic-butter finger rolls

These biscuit-like rolls are just a little garlicky and quite buttery. They're as fast to make as biscuits, but they don't keep, so eat them while they're hot. The rolls don't really need more butter, but some at your table might disagree, so be prepared.

MAKES 12 ROLLS

1. Set the oven to 450 degrees and adjust the rack position to the lower third.

2. Whack the garlic cloves with a mallet or smack them with the flat side of a chef's knife. Put the butter in an 8-x-8-x-2-inch baking pan and add the garlic. Slide the pan into the oven to melt the butter as the oven heats. When all the butter is melted, take the pan out of the oven. Spear the garlic cloves with a kitchen fork and stir them in the butter briefly to flavor it, then remove and discard the garlic. Keep the pan with the melted butter on the stovetop to stay warm while you make the rolls.

3. Using a whisk, mix the dry ingredients thoroughly in a bowl. Stir the milk in slowly with a fork until it's mixed in and you have a soft dough, about 30 strokes. Don't overmix.

4. Turn the dough out onto a well-floured board and knead lightly, about 10 times—the dough will be sticky.

5. Using a floured rolling pin, roll the dough out to a rectangle about 8 x 6 inches. Cut the dough into finger-size pieces with a floured sharp knife by making 6 long lengthwise slices, then cutting those in half to make 12 fingers. Put the rolls in the pan, rolling them to coat with the melted butter; they should almost touch each other.

6. Bake the rolls until golden brown, 15 to 20 minutes. Run a knife around the sides of the pan and remove the rolls with a spatula. Serve immediately.

- 3 garlic cloves, peeled
- 5⅓ tablespoons butter
- 2¼ cups all-purpose flour, plus more for dusting
- 1 tablespoon sugar
- 1 tablespoon plus ½ teaspoon baking powder
- 1½ teaspoons salt
- 1 cup milk

banana bread

I can promise you that just about everyone who tastes this is going to ask you for the recipe—it's that much better than other banana breads. It has more bananas than most. I also add nutmeg, and I like to mix in pecans or walnuts, but you can skip them. Just be sure the bananas are brown all over, really ripe.

Some people like cream cheese or butter smeared on slices of banana bread, but this one really doesn't need a thing. MAKES 1 LOAF

1. Set the oven to 350 degrees. Butter and flour a 9-x-5-x-4-inch loaf pan, or spray all over with baking spray.

2. In a small bowl, whisk together the flour, baking soda, and salt. Stir in the nuts if you're using them.

3. Mash the bananas very well with a wooden spoon in a large bowl, or use an electric mixer. Add the butter, sugar, eggs, and nutmeg to the bananas and mix well with an electric mixer on medium-high. On low speed, add the dry ingredients and mix thoroughly. Scrape the batter into the loaf pan.

4. Slide the pan into the oven. After 1 hour, start testing with a toothpick inserted into the center of the loaf. It will come out clean when the banana bread is done, probably about 1 hour and 15 minutes. Remove from the oven and cool on a rack, still in the loaf pan, for 10 minutes.

5. Run a knife around the edges of the pan and turn the banana bread out onto a platter to cool. Don't try to slice the loaf until it's cooled all the way. Wrapped in aluminum foil, the bread will keep for several days, or you can freeze it. Serve at room temperature.

1¼ cups all-purpose flour

1 teaspoon baking soda

½ teaspoon salt

½ cup chopped pecans or walnuts (optional)

5 very ripe bananas

1 stick (8 tablespoons) butter, softened

1 cup sugar

2 large eggs, lightly beaten with a fork

½ teaspoon grated nutmeg

monkey bread

Aunt Laura remembers making monkey bread back in the forties and fifties. I got intrigued with the idea and started experimenting. When I made monkey bread with my great-nephew Greg, he loved it so much he decided it was going to be his signature recipe.

You can't help but love monkey bread, because it's so much fun. It looks like a coffee cake, but then you pull little bits of it apart with your fingers, and they're all covered with delicious cinnamon sugar glaze. Kids love to help make this recipe.

The easiest way to make monkey bread is with supermarket buttermilk biscuits in the tube, but it's better made with frozen bread dough (also from the supermarket) and best of all made with the buttery dough I use for cinnamon rolls.

MAKES 1 LARGE COFFEE CAKE

1. Set the oven to 350 degrees. Spray a Bundt pan with baking spray.

2. If you are using dough, pull off pieces of dough and shape into golf ball–size balls.

3. Pour the melted butter into a shallow dish. Put the sugar and cinnamon in a large paper or plastic bag and shake well to mix.

4. Sprinkle half the nuts in the bottom of the Bundt pan. Working with a few balls of dough at a time, roll them in the melted butter, drop them into the cinnamon-sugar bag, and shake well to coat. Arrange the balls evenly in the Bundt pan, continuing until you have added half the balls. Drizzle with half the butter from the cake pan and sprinkle with the remaining pecans.

5. Coat the remaining dough balls and arrange them in the pan. Drizzle with the rest of the butter and scatter any leftover cinnamon sugar on top.

6. Bake until the top of the bread springs back when touched and a tester inserted comes out clean, 20 to 25 minutes. Let cool on a rack for 10 minutes, then turn the monkey bread out onto a plate and serve warm.

2 (4.5-ounce) tubes Pillsbury buttermilk biscuits (not the flaky ones), each biscuit quartered and shaped into balls

or

1 pound frozen bread dough, defrosted, allowed to rise in a warm place for 1 hour, covered with a tea towel

or

1 recipe Cinnamon Roll Dough (page 49), allowed to rise in a warm place for 1 hour, covered with a tea towel

1½ sticks (12 tablespoons) butter, melted

1¼ cups sugar

2 tablespoons ground cinnamon

½ cup chopped pecans

what's for dinner?

WHAT'S FOR DINNER? I know that question so well. My oldest grandson, Keo, lives with me, and several times a week his three younger brothers join him at my house for dinner when my daughter is working late. The big question is whether we'll have a one-pot dinner or what I call a two-pot dinner, which will stretch over two days. If I'm cooking for five of us, I want to make a lot so I'll be able to just heat it up the next day, but the younger boys want something they'll eat only once, no leftovers. They're always looking for a chance to lobby for their favorites, like Baked Spaghetti (page 169).

The second-oldest, Brandon, could eat peas and rice forever. In fact, almost everything my grandmother cooked makes Brandon happy, and if I've inspired a budding cook among these good-eater boys, it will be Brandon, who's curious about food and flavors and likes to help out in the kitchen.

I love the old favorites too, but I'm always looking for new tastes and new ideas, which are usually off the menu for the younger boys. An exception is Chicken-Fried Chicken, with its little zing of dried mint, which everyone loves. Most of the recipes here fall into the old-favorites category, but there are also some new favorites, like Potato-Chip Chicken and fast Roast Chicken in a Skillet.

I love the tradition of a good home-cooked family dinner with everyone at the table, blessing the food. But I also know that lots of times people just can't do that. That's sometimes true for me too. We all live in the real world, with its

jam-packed schedules and urgent obligations. If I've been running around all day, it may have to be pizza and a salad. For the boys, that's a big treat, not a compromise. Even if it's takeout, though, you don't have to give up your family dinner. Just one homemade thing can make a big difference. Take a few minutes to throw together some Sprightly Biscuits (page 77) for that one fresh-baked treat, make a salad (or let the kids do it), and gather everyone together to share the meal and talk about the day, and you've still got the heart of it. Some good fresh fruit in season for dessert puts a sweet but healthy taste in everyone's mouth with no effort from the cook, and it's a good habit to get into for the young ones.

For a knockout dinner, such as for a birthday, most people I know will go for the Awesome Fried Spareribs, which is probably my signature recipe. But if you have an electric fryer and you can remember to season the ribs the day (or even just a few hours) before, this huge treat can be a weekday dinner on a special day. When the answer to "What's for Dinner?" is those ribs, you can expect lots of whoops and hollers of pure joy.

tomato pie

I haven't met anybody who doesn't love tomato pie. It's one of those dishes you can play with, and I like to take it in an Italian direction, with basil and olive oil and Parmesan cheese. You know this recipe is still Southern, though, because it's got a Bisquick crust on the bottom and a cheesy mayonnaise crust on top.

Really ripe garden tomatoes are what you want for this recipe, but if you have a craving and it's the middle of winter, you could always use those Campari hothouse tomatoes on the vine from the supermarket.

This pie is rich and satisfying enough that all you need to serve with it is a sharp green salad—arugula goes really well with it. **SERVES 6 TO 8**

1. Drain the tomato slices in a single layer between paper towels until they stop oozing liquid, changing the paper towels if you need to. Or you can let them drain on a rack in a single layer over a baking sheet for 1 hour. In either case, pat dry with more paper towels.

2. Set the oven to 400 degrees. Have ready a 9-inch deep-dish pie plate.

3. In a medium bowl, use a fork to combine the Bisquick with the milk—you want it to barely hold together. Mix in the green onions. Knead the dough lightly, then press it evenly into the bottom of the pie plate and up the sides.

4. Salt and pepper the tomatoes. Arrange them in layers in the crust, scattering some of the basil leaves evenly over each layer, adding more pepper and drizzling a little, just a little, olive oil over each layer.

5. In a medium bowl, mix together the mayonnaise, cheese, and garlic with a fork. Spread the mixture evenly over the tomatoes with a thin spatula. The topping doesn't need to go all the way to the crust—you can leave a little edge of tomatoes showing.

4–6 medium garden-ripe tomatoes, sliced about ⅓ inch thick (see Tips)

2 cups Bisquick

½ cup milk

½ cup sliced green onions (scallions), including white and firm green parts

Salt and ground black pepper to taste

About 10 fresh basil leaves, torn

1 teaspoon extra-virgin olive oil, for drizzling

⅔ cup mayonnaise, preferably Duke's (see Sources, page 263)

½ cup shredded Parmesan cheese (not grated; see Tips)

1 garlic clove, pressed or minced

> **TIP**
> If you're using Campari tomatoes, you'll need about 16, from a 2-pound box.

continued...

6. Slide the pie into the oven and bake until golden brown on top, 30 to 35 minutes. Let the pie rest at least 10 minutes before serving warm.

TIPS

• You'll know after you arrange one layer of tomato slices in the pie plate how many layers you're going to have, so you can calculate how many basil leaves to save for the next layer (or layers).

• Instead of using tomato slices, you can dice, salt, and drain the tomatoes in a colander set over a bowl (instead of using the paper towel routine). Stir them up several times while they're draining to encourage the tomato water to leave. Save the liquid to drink or use in stews or soups. Spread all the tomatoes in the crust, sprinkle the torn basil leaves on top, and drizzle with the olive oil.

• You don't have to use Parmesan cheese; very sharp cheddar is classic. Whichever one you use, it's best if you shred the cheese yourself, using the big holes on a box grater.

• If you're serving the pie at the table and you grow your own basil, pluck a basil crown with a couple of layers of leaves from one of your plants and tuck the stem into the center of the pie before serving.

• The baked pie freezes perfectly. Thaw to room temperature before reheating slices in the microwave for about 30 seconds. Any more heating than that and you risk melting the mayonnaise and cheese, which will make a soggy mess.

TIP

You can use a regular pie-crust instead of Bisquick and just scatter the green onions over it before adding the tomato slices.

secret-weapon turkey wings

The secret weapon here is sweet Spanish smoked paprika. Make an effort to find it if you don't already have it on hand (see Sources, page 263), and I promise you'll be using it all the time as your secret weapon.

Turkey wings have a huge amount of flavor, especially if they're cooked long and slow. Once this dish is in the oven, you don't have to do a thing to it, so you're free for at least 2½ hours before dinner. **SERVES 6 TO 8**

1. Set the oven to 300 degrees. Have ready a large covered casserole dish (see Tip) or a Dutch oven.

2. Rinse the turkey pieces and put them in a large bowl. Sprinkle the Savannah seasoning over the wet wings and rub it in well.

3. Scatter about a third of the onion slices and green pepper in the casserole dish. Tuck all the turkey wings into the dish, and pour any liquid left at the bottom of the bowl over them. Drizzle the olive oil on top. Scatter the garlic over the turkey wings and sprinkle the paprika on top. Drizzle the Worcestershire over them. Scatter the remaining vegetables on top and pour the water evenly over everything.

4. Cover the dish and slide it into the oven. Cook until the thickest part of the biggest turkey wing tests tender when you try it with a cooking fork, 2½ to 3 hours. Serve.

2½ pounds turkey wings, each disjointed into 2 parts

1 tablespoon Dora's Savannah Seasoning (page 79)

1 medium onion, cut in half and sliced thin

⅓ large green bell pepper, sliced thin

2 tablespoons extra-virgin olive oil

1 garlic clove, chopped

1 teaspoon sweet Spanish smoked paprika (see Sources, page 263) or regular paprika

2 scant tablespoons Worcestershire sauce

1 cup water

TIP

If you're using a casserole dish, a squarish one will work best for holding all the turkey wings.

potato-chip chicken

This recipe sounds like it might be a joke, but it's really dynamite. Chicken drumsticks with a potato chip crust—what could be bad? Crunchcrunchcrunch, with tender succulent chicken under the crunch. After I tasted it at my friend Dorothy Lee's house, I had to get the recipe. It's fun to make, fun to eat, and as addictive as potato chips. And, of course, kids just love it.

You have to use rippled potato chips, and not low-salt or no-salt. Then you'll salt it all again—but don't worry, it's not too salty in the end. SERVES 6 OR MORE

1. Set the oven to 425 degrees and adjust the rack positions to the upper and lower thirds.

2. Massage the drumsticks with the Savannah seasoning and set aside.

3. Put half the potato chips into a food processor, along with 1 teaspoon of the salt. Grind into medium crumbs, about 15 seconds, stopping at least once to stir up the chips. Put the crumbs in a large shallow dish and repeat with the remaining chips and 1 teaspoon salt. Add to the bowl.

4. Now things get a little messy, so put down some newspaper on your counter. Put the flour in one large shallow dish and the beaten eggs in another. Make an assembly line, with the potato chip crumbs at the end. Have ready two baking sheets with racks perched on top.

5. Dip one drumstick in the flour to cover, shake well, and dip it into the eggs, turning to coat. Then, finally, the drumstick goes into the potato chip crumbs—press them in so the drumstick is well covered, and set it on the rack on one baking sheet. Repeat these steps with the remaining drumsticks.

6. Bake the chicken for 20 minutes and rotate the baking sheets. Bake for 10 to 20 more minutes, and then test one drumstick at the thickest point with a skewer. If the juices run

12 chicken drumsticks, rinsed and patted dry

1 teaspoon Dora's Savannah Seasoning (page 79)

1 (9.5-ounce) bag rippled potato chips

2 teaspoons salt

½ cup self-rising flour

2 large eggs, beaten with 1 tablespoon water with a fork

TIP

You can use 12 chicken thighs instead of drumsticks if you'd rather. The cooking time is the same.

clear, it's done. If not, keep cooking and testing every 10 minutes until the juices run clear.

7. Serve hot or warm.

dora says

I find myself giving the same advice to cooks over and over again, so I may as well give it to you too.

• **Take your time.** This is an essential part of cooking really good food. Read through the recipe and set everything out that you're going to need. If the butter needs to be softened, if the eggs need to be at room temperature, remember to account for the extra time. Think about what dish you're going to serve the food in and get it out and ready. Part of what makes people freak out about cooking is the pressure they put on themselves when they're not prepared.

• **Always save bacon grease, in a covered jar or grease container.** This is a great flavor booster for pan gravy, greens, almost anything. Save chicken-frying grease the same way, labeled and dated, because it doesn't last forever. It's great for greens and hoecakes.

• **Pay attention to your meat.** I want you to really *look* at it when you're getting ready to cook it, to trim off extra fat or little bits that don't belong there. Usually you need to rinse it so the seasoning will stick, and then you want to do that carefully, so the seasoning covers the meat evenly and well. It always makes me glad to see a pan of properly prepared pieces of meat lined up and ready to go into the oven, *looking good*.

• **Pay attention to your seasoning too.** If there's one thing that points up the difference between black and white Southern cooking, it's seasoning. Black cooks are always thinking about their seasoning, and many of them have their own special blends, just like I do. Good Southern cooking is bursting with flavor, and yours should be too.

• **It's a good idea to buy new spices and herbs just before Thanksgiving, when they come into the markets very fresh.** Red peppers like cayenne and paprika lose their spark quickly—a year is a long time for ground red pepper—so taste to be sure. Buy in bulk at markets that sell spices and herbs in bins—Frontier is a good brand, at Whole Foods and other markets—and put them in your old labeled jars. You'll save a huge amount of money that way and have really flavorful seasonings at the same time.

• **Taste, taste, taste, and correct the flavors as you go.** You want your food to be well balanced so no one element is screaming or missing the mark. If it's not right, check for salt, acid, sweetness, spiciness, and, sometimes, smokiness.

• **Don't be a robot and follow the cooking times in a recipe exactly.** My oven temperature may not be what yours is, so always check in good time, before things are supposed to be done, to see if they're still on course. Just

the way all ovens are different, all pans are different, and you need to use your eyes, your nose, and sometimes your fingers to decide whether things are done or need more—or less—time.

• **Sometimes you do all that and your dish just won't quite come together.** Try a little pat of butter, which carries flavor. If that doesn't work, bring another of my secret weapons: a

squeeze bottle of Parkay liquid margarine. A squeeze or two should do it. I have no idea why, but this trick has saved me lots of times when all my other efforts failed.

• **Very important: Have fun and enjoy yourself in the kitchen.** Put on your favorite music and let it inspire you. I cook to gospel music.

roast chicken under a skillet

What makes this chicken so good is roasting it in a very hot oven between two cast-iron skillets of the same size. But just one skillet will work too, as will a baking sheet with a rack on top.

The chicken is butterflied, so it cooks flat and fast, which means the breast doesn't dry out before the legs are cooked through. And a butterflied chicken has maximum exposed skin to crisp. The chicken in the skillet will look like it's about to dance, with the drumsticks pointing out, or it's being very modest, with the drumsticks pointing in.

The chicken is seasoned with simple flavors—olive oil, garlic, orange zest, and maybe some rosemary or oregano, but using cast-iron skillets always brings out something more.

Get the butcher to remove the backbone from the chicken (and save it for making stock), and this becomes a completely no-fuss recipe. **SERVES 4 TO 6**

1. Set the oven to 500 degrees. Adjust the rack positions so there's at least 10 inches between them. Put two cast-iron skillets at least 10 inches in diameter in the oven, one on each rack, while it heats.

2. While the skillets are getting very hot, trim any extra fat on the chicken. Crack the breastbone so the chicken will lie flatter: With the palm of your hand over the breastbone, press down with the heel of your other hand until you hear the crack—don't be gentle. The legs will be pushed out to the sides, as will the wings.

3. In a small bowl, mix the garlic and orange zest into the olive oil. Add the salt and pepper. Using a pastry brush, brush the garlic oil all over both sides of the chicken. Sprinkle all over with the rosemary or oregano, if using. Tuck the wing tips under the wings, or clip them and save them (with the backbone) for making stock later.

1 (4-pound) chicken, backbone removed (see Tips)

3 garlic cloves, pressed or minced

Grated zest of ½ large orange

3 tablespoons extra-virgin olive oil

1 teaspoon salt

½ teaspoon freshly ground black pepper

1 tablespoon dried rosemary or oregano, crumbled (optional)

White wine or chicken stock and lemon juice, for the sauce (optional)

continued...

4. When the oven hits 500 degrees and the skillets are blazing hot, pull the lower rack out so you can slip your prepared chicken into that skillet. Carefully arrange the chicken skin side up in the skillet. Pull the other skillet out from its rack and place it squarely on top of the chicken—be careful! The skillets will be very hot, and the chicken will sizzle. Roast the chicken until the juices in the thigh run clear, about 45 minutes.

5. When the chicken is done, pull out the rack a little and lift off the top skillet—this way, it's not so heavy and you're less likely to drop it or burn yourself. Now slide out the skillet with the chicken in it and remove the chicken to a serving platter to rest for 5 minutes. Keep any juices in the skillet warm to pour over the sliced chicken.

6. If you'd like a sauce, add a little wine or chicken stock to the pan and scoop up the bits left in the bottom of the skillet. Taste the pan drippings for seasoning; if you used stock you might want to brighten them with a little lemon juice if you think they need it.

7. Carve the chicken. Drizzle the pan sauce, if you have it, over the chicken and serve.

TIP

If you have only one cast-iron skillet, you can use two bricks or even flat rocks. Cover with aluminum foil and put them in the oven to heat up with the skillet.

TIPS

• If you have the time, salt the chicken all over the night before you cook it and refrigerate it overnight on a rack over a baking sheet, covered. The flavor will bloom by morning. When you're ready to prepare the chicken the next day, skip the salt in the recipe.

• If there's no butcher to remove the backbone, here's how you do it: Get some poultry shears or good kitchen scissors and cut all the way down both sides of the backbone, then pull it out.

• You can season the chicken with paprika instead of rosemary or with Dora's Savannah Seasoning (page 79).

chicken-spaghetti casserole

This is an old-fashioned casserole made with chicken cooked in a tasty broth, combined with spaghetti, and sauced with sour cream and two cheeses. All this goodness bakes together for just 25 minutes, which means that you can prep all the ingredients a day ahead and just combine them shortly before you want to serve.

SERVES 4 TO 6

1. Put the chicken pieces and the gizzard and neck, if you have them, in a large pot. Add the celery, onion, green pepper, water, Savannah seasoning, bouillon cubes, and Accent, if using, and bring to a boil over high heat. Reduce the heat to medium-low, cover the pot, and simmer until the chicken is tender, about 1½ hours. When the chicken is done, remove the pieces to a baking sheet to cool. Set the pot aside.

2. When the chicken is cool, pull off the skin and pick the meat off the bones. Cut the meat into bite-sized pieces and set aside in a large bowl. Toss out the skin and bones.

3. Set the oven to 350 degrees. Butter an 8-inch square casserole dish.

4. Set a colander over a large bowl. Strain the broth into a clean pot and bring it to a boil. Add the spaghetti, stir well, and cook until al dente (barely tender). Drain the spaghetti in the colander set over the bowl.

5. Add 2 cups of the broth and 2 cups of the cooked spaghetti to the chicken (reserve the remaining broth and spaghetti. Stir in the sour cream, cheddar, ½ cup of the Colby Jack, and the eggs, mixing to combine.

6. Scoop the mixture into the casserole dish and bake until bubbly, about 25 minutes.

7. Remove the casserole from the oven and scatter the remaining ¼ cup Colby Jack cheese and the parsley, if you're using it, on top. Serve hot.

1 (3-pound) chicken, cut into pieces, with the gizzard and neck, if included, or about 3 pounds chicken parts

2 celery ribs, diced

1 medium onion, diced

1 large green bell pepper, diced

7 cups water

1 tablespoon plus 2 teaspoons Dora's Savannah Seasoning (page 79)

6 chicken bouillon cubes

1 tablespoon Accent (optional)

½ pound spaghetti, broken into bite-sized pieces

½ cup sour cream

1½ cups shredded cheddar cheese

¾ cup shredded Colby Jack cheese

2 large eggs, beaten with a fork

2 sprigs fresh parsley, chopped (optional)

dora's chicken

I'm not sure how this got so famous, but it just did. People love it as much as fried chicken, and it's much easier to fix, despite its complex taste. It's best to start the day before by seasoning the chicken (though you can also season it early in the morning on the day you plan to serve it). Then you add another layer of seasoning, which gives it great depth. The chicken cooks on top of a layer of onion rings and minced garlic, and it smells so good while it's cooking that people will start coming into the kitchen, asking when it's going to be ready.

You can use fat chicken wings or drumettes or thighs—they'll all be great—but choose just one cut, or the timing can get messed up. If you have any leftovers, the best way to serve them is to heat up the broth that comes off the chicken and serve them with grits—see the Tip. **SERVES 8 OR MORE**

1. The day before you plan to serve the chicken (or early in the morning of serving day), rinse the chicken pieces well and put them in a large bowl. Sprinkle the Savannah seasoning over them and mix with your hands to distribute the seasoning and massage it into the meat a bit. Cover and refrigerate overnight, or until you're ready to cook the chicken.

2. Set the oven to 350 degrees. Spray a large baking sheet well with olive oil spray.

3. Spread the onion rings evenly over the pan and sprinkle the garlic evenly on top. Arrange the chicken pieces evenly over the onions and garlic. (Don't tuck the wing tips under.) Sprinkle the rotisserie seasoning evenly over the chicken, followed by the blackening seasoning. Spray all over with olive oil spray.

4. Carefully add the water to the bottom of the pan—*not* over the chicken. Bake until the chicken is cooked through, about 45 minutes for wings, 1 hour for drumettes or thighs. This is one of those dishes that tastes best if the chicken is actually a little overcooked. Serve immediately.

16 fat whole chicken wings, 32 drumettes, or 16 chicken thighs

1 tablespoon Dora's Savannah Seasoning (page 79)

Extra-virgin olive oil in a spray bottle

1 medium onion, cut into rings

1 tablespoon minced garlic

2 tablespoons rotisserie seasoning (any brand)

2 tablespoons blackening seasoning (any brand)

1 cup water

TIP

Be sure to save the oniony broth in the bottom of the pan. It's delicious, and it makes a fine warm sauce to serve over grits with reheated leftover chicken.

chicken-fried chicken

Even if you've never tried chicken-fried steak, you've probably heard all about it—a pounded piece of steak double-breaded and fried crisp, often served with gravy. But Chicken-Fried Chicken is a newer arrival, at least where I live, and it's probably from the same source, the Lone Star State. It's thin pounded chicken breasts—chicken tenders work well too—cooked like the steak and always served with milk gravy. The classic is served with mashed potatoes, but I like it with rice. **SERVES 4**

1. To make the chicken: In a large shallow bowl, whisk the buttermilk with the garlic and paprika. Add the chicken and move the pieces around so that they're all covered with buttermilk. Put the chicken and buttermilk in a plastic freezer bag or in a container with a lid and massage the buttermilk all over the chicken. Let sit in the fridge overnight if you can, or for just a few hours, if that's all the time you have.

2. When you're ready to cook the chicken, mix the flour and Savannah seasoning in a medium bowl. Remove the chicken one piece at a time from the buttermilk, shaking it well, dredge it in the flour, shake off any extra flour, and put on a plate.

3. Heat the oil in a large heavy cast-iron skillet over medium-high heat until it's rippling. Add the chicken carefully—don't crowd the pan. You'll probably need to do this in batches, so scoop out any flour that's fallen off into the oil between batches so it won't burn. Fry until the chicken is golden brown all over, about 4 minutes for each side. Drain on paper towels and keep warm under a loose foil tent while you make the gravy.

4. To make the gravy: Pour out all but 1½ tablespoons vegetable oil from the pan and heat over medium-high heat. Whisk in the flour until smooth. Whisk in 1 cup of the milk and cook, stirring, until the mixture thickens. Whisk in the second cup of milk. Stir in the mint and simmer for 2 to 3 minutes. Return the chicken to the gravy and add the onion. Cover the skillet and simmer for 10 minutes.

Chicken

- 1 cup buttermilk
- 1 tablespoon granulated garlic
- ⅛ teaspoon sweet Spanish smoked paprika
- 4 skinless, boneless single chicken breasts (about 1 pound), sliced horizontally in half and rolled thin with a rolling pin or pounded with a meat mallet (see Tips)
- 1 cup all-purpose flour
- ¼ cup Dora's Savannah Seasoning (page 79)
- ½ cup vegetable oil, for frying

Milk Gravy

- 1½ tablespoons all-purpose flour
- 2 cups milk
- 1 teaspoon Dora's Savannah Seasoning (page 79)
- ½ teaspoon dried mint
- 1 small onion, sliced into rings

5. With a slotted spoon, transfer the chicken to a platter. Serve immediately, with the gravy on the side.

> **TIPS**
>
> • What you want for the chicken is skinless, boneless pieces of breast about ¼ inch thick. Single chicken breasts cut horizontally in half, as called for in this recipe, will do it. Or look at the supermarket for something labeled chicken fillets or thin-sliced chicken cutlets or chicken tenderloins. If they're thicker than ¼ inch in places, you'll need to pound them with a meat mallet or rolling pin between sheets of wax paper so they're flat, or get the butcher to do it.
>
> • Chicken tenders, which are smaller than breasts and come from a muscle just under the breast, work fine too. Don't worry about the white line on chicken tenders. It's like those little white strings inside eggs—they disappear when they're cooked.

killer fried pork chops

I don't say "killer" lightly. These tender, beautiful chops have a crisp golden brown coating you can't wait to bite into. If you've ever had trouble producing a great, moist pork chop, this recipe is for you. The chops will taste best when you've treated them with care, rubbing the seasoning in evenly and well.

People really love center-cut on-the-bone chops, so that's what I buy.   SERVES 4

1. Rinse the chops well and drain. Sprinkle the scant tablespoon of the Savannah seasoning evenly over both sides of the chops and rub it in well.

2. In a shallow bowl wide enough for dipping the chops, beat the buttermilk and egg with a whisk.

3. Put the flour and the remaining 1 teaspoon seasoning into a brown paper bag or plastic bag.

4. Begin heating the Crisco in a large cast-iron skillet over medium-high heat—you want about ¾ inch of fat in the pan, so add more if you need it. Meantime, dip the chops one by one into the buttermilk mixture, then drop into the bag with the flour and shake well, coating the entire chop. Shake off any excess flour and put the chop on a plate.

5. When the oil is hot—a deep-fry thermometer should read 365 degrees—carefully lower the chops into the skillet. Fry the chops until golden brown on one side, about 4 minutes, then turn to brown on the other side, another 4 minutes. Remove the chops with tongs, shaking off any excess oil, and drain on paper towels. Serve immediately.

4 bone-in center-cut pork chops, about 1 inch thick

1 scant tablespoon plus 1 teaspoon Dora's Savannah Seasoning (page 79)

½ cup buttermilk

1 large egg

1 cup self-rising flour

1 cup Crisco, or more if needed

> **TIP**
>
> Of course you should save the frying oil. Pour it into a little jar or glass measuring cup to cool. Then be sure to scrape up all the good crunchy bits in the pan—the drippings—that come from crumbs of coating falling off the pork chops during frying. I like to save the drippings separately and stir them into pan gravy like little flavor bombs.

> **TIP**
>
> If you have any leftover pork chops, you can make Smothered Pork Chops (recipe follows) the next day. Or just double the Fried Pork Chop recipe if that's your plan so you have 4 leftover chops.

smothered pork chops

These chops are so good that I often make a double batch of my Killer Fried Pork Chops so I can make them. All you do is slice the cold pork chops and then simmer the meat a bit in spiced-up pan gravy. Leftovers never had it so good.

Serve the smothered chops over mashed or scalloped potatoes or rice. **SERVES 4**

1. Pour the frying oil into a heavy skillet; keep the drippings aside for now. Heat the oil over medium heat. When it's hot, lower the heat to medium-low and stir in the flour with a whisk—do this *slowly*, or the mixture can get bitter and lumpy. Add the drippings and continue to whisk until it all browns a little.

2. Add the Savannah seasoning and whisk the gravy base until it's the color of coffee with cream, then add the onion and pepper strips, along with as much of the water as you think you'll need to make a loose gravy, starting with 2 cups. Cook, stirring, until the gravy thickens. If it gets too thick, add more water.

3. Add the pork chop strips, cover, and simmer for 20 minutes, still over medium-low heat, checking occasionally to be sure the gravy's not getting too thick and adding water if it is. Serve hot.

⅓ cup leftover frying oil and drippings from Killer Fried Pork Chops (see Tip, page 113)

½ cup all-purpose flour

1 tablespoon Dora's Savannah Seasoning (page 79)

½ onion, cut in half and sliced thin

½ medium green bell pepper, cut into thin strips

2–3 cups water

4 Killer Fried Pork Chops (page 113), cut off the bone in strips

> **TIP**
>
> The secret to great gravy is not only tasty drippings, but taking the time to cook it slowly over heat that's not too high. Don't be in a rush!

soul food

Not everyone agrees on the precise definition of "soul food," but it's just what it says: food for your soul. A lot of the recipes in this book, like fried chicken and cornbread and collard greens and sweet potato pie, might be called soul food, but for me what I really crave is a smoky and spicy combination. It includes more than barbecue, and it often involves meat with the bones in so you can work your way around them and pick up that sweet meat by the bone.

I know a lot of people like to go out to soul food joints with their friends, but to me it's never as good as it is at home. For one thing, everyone's food comes at a different time, and people get mad about that, and maybe some things are really good and others are just nasty. You get something to eat, but your soul doesn't.

If you're not used to making this kind of meal, invite people over for potluck. Ask them to bring something to go with what you're cooking, something they think of as soul food. I think you'll all be surprised at how great it all tastes, and before you know it, you'll be famous for your soul food dinners. If you want to send everyone at the table over the moon, make Awesome Fried Spareribs (page 117)—no soul food joint can match them.

A soul food dinner also means cornbread on the table, greens and rice, and plenty of desserts to sample—sweet potato pie, banana pudding, maybe red velvet cake or peach cobbler. Now your soul is happy—and you might want to add a bowl of tangerines or strawberries to the dessert table for the body too.

awesome fried spareribs

If you've never heard of fried spareribs, that's probably because you haven't eaten at my house. Back in the mid-1990s, I found myself getting tired of cooking ribs on the grill, delicious as they were. I had the idea to fry them and I tried it, even though it seemed like frying fatty ribs might be a really bad plan. But what actually happens if you do it right is, well, awesome. The ribs lose some of their inner fat in the process, and they become dry and crisp outside and succulent inside. These ribs are now my most requested dish, with friends and family begging me to make them for their birthdays and any other occasion they can think of that might persuade me.

You need to start the day before and let the ribs season overnight to get the flavor into the meat, not just on top of it. For frying, you'll need a deep fryer or a Dutch oven with a fryer basket (see Tip). Once you start frying the ribs, their aroma will take over the house and people will start begging for them as they're cooked. It's okay to eat as you go along, but be careful—a big eater can eat most of the ribs before dinner's even served. A way around that is to ask the butcher at the supermarket to cut the racks of ribs horizontally in half, so people can have a half-rib taste—perfect for a party.

I like to serve the ribs with turnip greens and rice and cornbread, and it's one of my favorite meals. SERVES 6 TO 8

1. Start the recipe the night before you plan to serve the ribs: If you didn't get the butcher to trim the ribs, you'll want to remove the flap at the bottom of the ribs and the extra bone at the top, the big backbone. Cut the trimmed ribs into single-rib pieces. You can cook the trimmed parts too if you cut them into bite-sized pieces.

2. Rinse the meat and let it drain in a colander, then season the ribs with the Savannah seasoning and rub it in well. Put the seasoned ribs into a large bowl or pan, cover, and refrigerate overnight.

3. The next day, when you're ready to cook, have ready racks set on a couple of baking sheets for draining the ribs. Fill a deep fryer with oil to the maximum line or a Dutch oven with

2 large slabs spareribs, about 5½ pounds each

2 tablespoons Dora's Savannah Seasoning (page 79)

Vegetable oil, for frying

2 cups self-rising flour

about 4 inches of oil—but not more than one third of the way up the sides of the pot. Set the fryer temperature for 365 degrees, or use a deep-fry thermometer in the Dutch oven.

4. While the oil is heating up, put the flour in a brown paper bag or a plastic bag. Working with 5 ribs at a time, shake them in the bag of flour, pressing down on the outside of the bag to get the flour to adhere to the meat so you'll get a good crust. Then shake the ribs as they come out of the bag, so no extra flour will fall off and burn during the frying, and lower them directly into the fryer or pot once you're ready to fry.

5. Check to be sure the temperature is right at 365 degrees. Throw in a little flour and if it sizzles, the oil is ready. Lower the ribs slowly into the hot oil—don't crowd them—and fry until golden brown, 15 to 20 minutes. Drain on the racks and serve right away, or keep warm until all the ribs are cooked.

6. Save any leftovers for Smothered Ribs (recipe below).

TIP

If you don't have a fryer basket, use tongs or a slotted spoon to lower the ribs into the hot oil and then to lift them out when they're done.

smothered ribs

MAKES 3 TO 4 CUPS GRAVY

½ cup frying oil
1 cup seasoned flour
1 tablespoon Dora's Savannah Seasoning (page 79)
1 large onion, sliced thin
4¼ cups hot water
Salt and pepper to taste
Leftover awesome fried spareribs

Save the leftover frying oil and the seasoned flour and make smothered ribs. Heat the frying oil over medium heat. Mix the seasoned flour and Savannah seasoning and stir it into the oil. Add the onion, and hot water. Cook, stirring, until it thickens and season with salt and pepper. Add the leftover ribs or the meat and simmer for 30 minutes.

baby back ribs

If you're not up for the whole frying routine, these are the ribs to make—they're quick to prepare and the oven does the rest. But they taste deeply seasoned, not like shortcut ribs at all. And if you line the baking sheet with foil, the cleanup will be simple too. **SERVES 4**

1. Set the oven to 350 degrees. Line a baking sheet with foil.

2. Put the slab of ribs on the baking sheet. Mix the remaining ingredients except for the olive oil together, then turn the ribs meaty side up and rub the mixture well into both sides, starting with the bony side. Drizzle the olive oil evenly over the top of the slab.

3. Bake the ribs until they are fall-off-the-bone tender, about 1½ hours. Let rest at room temperature for 10 minutes, then cut into 2-rib serving pieces and serve warm.

1 slab baby back ribs, about 2½ pounds (10–12 ribs)

1 tablespoon Dora's Savannah Seasoning (page 79)

1 tablespoon rosemary garlic seasoning (see Tips)

½ teaspoon crushed red pepper

½ teaspoon freshly ground black pepper

1 tablespoon extra-virgin olive oil

TIPS

• Look for meaty ribs. They will be more expensive, but warehouse clubs often have them at a good price.

• You can buy rosemary garlic seasoning or you can make your own, using about 1½ teaspoons crumbled dried rosemary and the same amount of granulated garlic. Multiply the seasoning ingredients and keep in a jar marked "Baby Back Ribs," and you can put together this dish in about 3 minutes. The mixture will keep at least 3 months, but give it a good sniff before you use it to be sure it's still potent.

stews

ALMOST EVERYTHING I COOK IS SLOW-COOKED, to bring out the flavors, but the dishes in this chapter really depend on long, slow simmering. They're perfect for late fall and winter in the Lowcountry, when it's cold enough that you want to warm up with something that's been bubbling for hours, sending fragrant hints of the delicious food to come all through the house.

One good thing about stews is that they always taste better the next day, after the flavors have all had a chance to get acquainted—which makes life a lot easier for the cook. Be sure to taste the stews once they're reheated—they may need a little more seasoning. Or they might just need a little sprinkle of chopped fresh parsley to look their best.

daddy's catfish stew

When my stepmother, Sexy, came home with a big haul of catfish after a good day's fishing, my Daddy would make his special catfish stew. Sally would clean the fish and take out the sharp pointy neck bone with pliers, but leave in the rest of the bones. My father loved the heads of any fish; he always said that was the best part. But I don't like to be looking at the face of what I'm eating, and I especially don't want to stare it in the eye, so I use "dressed" fish—cleaned and no heads (see Tip).

Daddy would deep-fry the catfish, heads on, one at a time, and once the frying was done, he'd use the frying grease at the bottom of the pot to start his gravy for the fish, adding tomatoes, potatoes, carrots, and seasonings and simmering until it was just right. Then the fried fish would go for a swim in the gravy, making it into a hearty stew. We'd each get a whole fish to ourselves, with plenty of gravy, served over grits or rice. We *loved* that dinner. I still serve it today, over brown rice. It does the catfish proud.

If possible, start seasoning the fish the night before, or early in the morning of the day you will serve it. SERVES 4 TO 6

1. Up to a day ahead, sprinkle the catfish evenly inside and out with 2 tablespoons of the salt and 1½ teaspoons of the pepper. Put the catfish on a platter and wrap in plastic wrap. Refrigerate for at least 2 hours, or overnight.

2. Pat the catfish dry. Heat about an inch of oil, with the bacon grease, if you have it, in a large cast-iron skillet over medium-high heat. Once it's hot, fry the catfish in batches until golden brown on both sides, 8 to 10 minutes total. Remove the catfish to a platter and set aside.

3. Pour off all but ¼ cup of the oil from the pan and stir in the tomatoes (not the juice), garlic, the remaining 1 tablespoon salt and 1½ teaspoons pepper, and the sugar. Cook over medium heat for 5 minutes, stirring from time to time.

4. Scrape the contents of the skillet into a Dutch oven. Add the 6 cups water and some of the tomato juice, about ½ cup. Bring to a boil over medium heat and add the potatoes. Return to a

5 whole medium dressed catfish (about ½ pound each; see Tip)

3 tablespoons salt

1 tablespoon ground black pepper

Vegetable oil, plus a little bacon grease if you have it, for frying

4 canned peeled plum tomatoes, drained (save the juice) and cut into quarters

1 tablespoon minced garlic

1½ teaspoons sugar

6 cups plus 2 tablespoons water

5 medium russet potatoes, peeled, cut lengthwise in half and then crosswise into thirds

8 carrots, cut into 1-inch chunks

boil and boil for 5 minutes, then add the carrots, onions, and celery.

5. Meantime, in a small bowl or teacup, mix the flour and the remaining 2 tablespoons water with a fork until smooth. Thicken the cooking liquid by adding a little of the flour mixture in several places, here and there, whisking it in immediately with the fork so it doesn't get lumpy. If the liquid still seems too thin, repeat with more of the flour mixture.

6. Stir in the butter and add the catfish to the pot. Cover and let it all simmer down over medium heat for 20 to 25 minutes, until all the vegetables are tender. Serve over hot rice or grits, with all the gravy spooned on top.

1 medium onion, cut into 6 wedges

4 celery ribs, cut on an angle into 1-inch chunks

1½ tablespoons all-purpose flour

½ stick (4 tablespoons) butter

Rice or grits, for serving

TIP

For my recipes, I like to use a gutted, skinned, headless fish that still has the bones in—a dressed catfish. Unless you are buying fillets, be sure to ask your fishmonger to remove the barb at the top of the spine just behind the head. I can tell you from childhood experience that that barb is painful if it goes through your skin, and the pain can last for days.

chicken brunswick stew

This is one of those famous old Southern dishes people fight over: Is it from Brunswick, Georgia, or Brunswick, Virginia? Does it have tomatoes in it—and squirrel or pork? Does it have to cook all day and all night? Some of the versions with everything that walks around tossed into them are too much for me. I like it with just chicken, which is the one essential meat—corn is the other essential. There's a tradition in some areas that it goes with barbecue, which seems like overkill. But it's very good, so maybe it goes with everything.

You can serve the stew by itself in a big bowl or over rice or grits. It's a great dish for picky eaters, like my grandson Keo, who can't get enough of it even though he usually hates onions and peppers. **SERVES 4 TO 6**

1. Put the chicken, water, and Savannah seasoning in a large pot over medium-high heat. Add the bouillon cubes and stir to mix in the seasoning. Put the lid on and once it comes to a boil, turn the heat down to a simmer and cook for about an hour, or until the meat is falling off the bone. Remove the chicken. When the chicken is cool enough, pull the meat from the bones and shred it, using tongs and your fingers. Throw out the skin and bones.

2. Bring the broth back to a simmer, return the shredded chicken to the pot, and add all the remaining ingredients (except the rice or grits). Let it simmer, uncovered, for another half hour.

3. Taste for seasoning—it could need more pepper or salt or more hot sauce. Serve in individual bowls or over warm rice or grits.

- 2 whole bone-in chicken breasts, or 4 bone-in chicken breast halves, rinsed (or use leftovers; see Tip)
- 8 cups water
- 1 tablespoon Dora's Savannah Seasoning (page 79)
- 4 chicken bouillon cubes
- ½ cup coarsely chopped onion
- ½ cup coarsely chopped green or red bell pepper
- 1 (14.75-ounce) can whole-kernel corn
- 1 (15.25-ounce) can creamed corn
- 1 (32-ounce) can diced tomatoes
- ½ teaspoon ground black pepper, or more to taste
- ⅓ cup Kraft BBQ sauce (or homemade; page 132)
- 1 teaspoon Texas Pete hot sauce or Tabasco, or more to taste
- 2 tablespoons butter

  Foolproof Rice (page 220) or cooked grits, for serving

TIP

If you have leftover cooked chicken, you can use it here. You'll need 3 to 4 cups shredded chicken. Just mix together the water, bouillon cubes or chicken base, and Savannah seasoning in the pot, then add the shredded chicken along with all the other ingredients and simmer together for about 30 minutes.

oxtail stew

You may not see a lot of oxtails on your local menus, but here in Savannah they out-sell fried chicken—and I've heard the same thing about Atlanta. Daddy loved a good oxtail stew, and he taught me to pass up the oxtails with yellow fat—they're old, and they can take forever to get tender. Not that you shouldn't cook them a long time. I like to cook them very slowly over many hours, even overnight. Then the next day you can easily peel off any fat that's accumulated on top of the chilled stew.

In our family we never served oxtail stew without rice, and it was always Converted (parboiled) rice, rinsed until the water ran clear to get rid of extra starch. Some people use cornstarch to thicken the gravy, but I don't; I stick with old-fashioned flour-thickened gravy. SERVES 6

1. You have a choice here: You can cook the oxtails for 2½ to 3 hours at 350 degrees, or you can cook them all day or overnight at 200 degrees. Set the oven according to your plan.

2. Put the oxtails in a large bowl. Sprinkle them with the Savannah seasoning and Accent, if you're using it, and work the seasoning in evenly using your hands.

3. Put the bouillon cubes in a 3-quart casserole dish with a lid and add a layer of the onion and bell pepper. Arrange the seasoned oxtails evenly on top. Drizzle the Worcestershire sauce and melted butter on top and add 3 cups water if you're cooking at 350 degrees, or 2 cups if you're cooking at 200 degrees. Cover the casserole and put it in the oven.

4. If you're cooking at the higher temperature, check to see if the oxtails are tender after 2½ hours—they should be falling off the bones, which may take another half hour. If you're cooking at 200 degrees, test after 8 to 10 hours. (If you have time, chill the stew once it's cooked and then remove the fat on top before reheating.)

5. To make the gravy, spoon off any extra fat from the stew and transfer the oxtails and vegetables to a platter. Pour the

5½ pounds oxtails (with no yellow fat), rinsed

1 tablespoon plus 1 teaspoon Dora's Savannah Seasoning (page 79)

2 teaspoons Accent (optional)

4 beef bouillon cubes

1 medium onion, sliced thin

½ large green or red bell pepper, sliced thin

2 tablespoons Worcestershire sauce

2 tablespoons butter, melted

2 or 3 cups water, plus 1 tablespoon

2 tablespoons all-purpose flour

Foolproof Rice (page 220), for serving

broth from the casserole into a small saucepan and set over medium-high heat—you want it to be bubbling hot.

6. Meantime, in a small bowl, mix well the flour with the remaining 1 tablespoon water to make a slurry. When the broth is bubbling, whisk in the slurry and continue whisking until the gravy is thick and the flour taste is cooked out.

7. Serve the oxtails and vegetables over rice, with the gravy passed at the table.

> **TIP**
>
> Be sure to heat the broth for the gravy until it's bubbling hot, or you'll get some lumps when you add the flour slurry.

bop's pot roast with potatoes

My friend Bop makes a really tasty pot roast that takes just about 15 minutes to put together. You brown the meat first, and then everything cooks in the oven until you thicken the sauce at the end and serve it with a salad and some good bread. It couldn't be simpler. Of course, like all pot roasts, it's better the next day.

SERVES 8 TO 10

1. Set the oven to 350 degrees.

2. Mix together ¼ cup of the flour, the salt, and pepper. Rub the seasoned flour all over the roast.

3. Heat a Dutch oven over medium-high heat and add the oil. When it's shimmering, brown the roast, turning it as it cooks to brown all sides.

4. Scatter the potatoes, green pepper, and onion around the roast. Pour 3 cups of the water around the roast and drop in the bouillon cubes. Cover the pot, transfer to the oven, and bake until the meat is fully tender, 2 to 2½ hours.

5. Remove the roast from the oven and move the roast and vegetables to a platter. Cover with foil to keep warm and let rest for 15 to 20 minutes.

6. While the meat is resting, pour off the broth from the Dutch oven into a saucepan. Put the saucepan over medium-high heat and bring the liquid to a boil.

7. Meantime, pour the remaining 1 cup water into a small bowl and whisk in the remaining 3 tablespoons flour to make a smooth slurry. Add the slurry to the boiling liquid slowly, whisking, and continue to whisk until the gravy is smooth and thickened and the flour taste is cooked out, 5 to 8 minutes.

8. Remove the meat to a carving board and slice. Return the slices to the platter, surround with the potatoes and vegetables, and pour the gravy over everything.

¼ cup plus 3 tablespoons all-purpose flour

1 teaspoon salt

½ teaspoon ground black pepper

1 (3-pound) boneless chuck roast, at room temperature

1 tablespoon vegetable oil

4 medium russet potatoes, peeled and quartered

1 medium green bell pepper, sliced thin

1 medium onion, cut in half and then sliced thin

4 cups water

3 beef bouillon cubes

TIPS

• You can leave out the potatoes and serve the meat and other vegetables over mashed potatoes.

• If you're making the pot roast a day ahead, stop at the point when the meat is tender. Cool in the pot and refrigerate overnight. When you're ready to serve, reheat the roast in the pot. Make the gravy just before serving.

pigs' feet in barbecue sauce

This dish is soul food for sure, and people who love it will be falling all over you with excitement when they hear you're cooking it. The barbecue sauce is sweet and spicy, and the pigs' feet are succulent, with some little bones to chew around. But not everyone has even considered eating a pig's foot, so have plenty of other food on the table if you've got some pig-foot virgins coming to dinner.

You need to be careful where you buy your pigs' feet. I get mine at an immaculate store in Savannah, and they have baby-pink skin and are really clean. Some places have good prices but the skin has browned and all the hair hasn't been removed— you don't want those at any price.

Serve with rice and cooked greens on the side. SERVES 4 TO 6

1. Put the pigs' feet in a large pot and cover with cold water. Add the vinegar and set the pot to boil over high heat.

2. When the pot boils, some scum will form on the top of the water. Put a colander in the sink and pour the water off the pigs' feet. Rinse the pigs' feet and the pot very well in hot water.

3. Put the feet back in the pot with the 5 cups hot water and the Savannah seasoning and Accent, if you're using it. Stir the seasoning in and bring the water to a rapid boil. Turn the heat down to a low simmer, so that just a few bubbles are coming up. Add the vegetables and Worcestershire sauce and stir well.

4. Now the little feet are bound for glory. Let them simmer slowly until very tender, almost falling off the bone, which can take anywhere from 1 to 2 hours.

5. **Meantime, make the barbecue sauce:** Cook all the ingredients down in a heavy, medium pot uncovered over low heat, stirring often, 45 minutes to 1 hour. Don't let the sauce get so hot it starts to pop—it should be a gentle heat that will slowly concentrate the sauce a bit. Once it's hot, taste it (it

- 2 pounds pigs' feet (2 or 3 feet; ask the butcher to cut them crosswise in half)
- ¼ cup distilled white vinegar
- 5 cups hot water
- 1 tablespoon Dora's Savannah Seasoning (page 79)
- 1 teaspoon Accent (optional)
- ½ medium green bell pepper, sliced thin
- ½ medium onion, sliced thin
- 2 tablespoons Worcestershire sauce

TIP

Store leftover barbecue sauce in a sealed jar in the refrigerator. It keeps for weeks, and it's great on ribs.

won't taste right until it's very hot and cooked down, so be careful) and see if you need a little more of something.

6. A little before the pigs' feet are done, set the oven to 350 degrees.

7. When the feet are done, scoop them out with a slotted spoon, along with the vegetables, into a casserole dish. Spoon 2 cups of the barbecue sauce evenly on top to glaze the pigs' feet and bake, uncovered, until the casserole is bubbly on the sides, 10 to 15 minutes.

8. Serve right away.

Ultimate Barbecue Sauce

- 5 cups light brown sugar
- 4 cups ketchup
- ½ cup plus 1 tablespoon Worcestershire sauce
- 1 tablespoon yellow mustard
- 1 lemon, rolled well on the countertop to soften and juiced
- 1½ teaspoons Dora's Savannah Seasoning (page 79)
- 1 teaspoon honey
- 2 teaspoons ground black pepper
- 2 teaspoons Texas Pete or other hot sauce

the catch

OUR RIVERS AND SEACOAST off Savannah and the Sea Islands give up some amazing fish, crab, shrimp, oysters, and other fantastic critters—even eels. Some of them are still free for the fishing or netting, and I learned all about that early, not only from my Daddy, but also, especially, from my stepmother, Sexy, who would fish all day, sunup to sundown, whenever she could. She knew where all the great fishing holes were, and she'd travel far away, hours away, to the best ones. She'd bring her daughter with her, and together they'd clean the fish they caught.

Sometimes she'd bring some of us along too, and my sister and I would hold our poles and stare into the dappled water in hopes of bringing up porgies or whitings or mullet or some other tasty fish, but Sexy always caught the most fish. Then that night she'd invite everyone to come over for a big fish fry and a huge garden salad at our house on Duffy Street. She loved to grow tomatoes and cucumbers, as well as green and red peppers, in her garden right in the middle of the city. You'd always see peppers growing in Savannah in the old days, especially killer-hot bird's-eye peppers, raised in a window box if you didn't have a garden.

As for what's taken from the waters along the coast, I have a new appreciation of what that has meant for the descendants of the Sea Island slaves, the Gullahs and Geechees, now that I've visited the Pin Point Heritage Museum, about twelve miles south of Savannah. After the Civil War, the slaves on those islands were free but they stayed on the Sea Islands and made a life for themselves using their skills with fish and seafood. On Ossabaw Island, there was a thriving community with the Hinder Me Not church. After a series of hurricanes in the 1880s and 1890s, though, they realized they should leave and come inland, and they settled, along with freed slaves from other Sea Islands, in Pin Point, an area on the Moon River, a tidal river Johnny Mercer made famous in the song about it.

Pin Point is beautiful, with live oak trees hung with moss, lovely marshes, and sparkling waters beyond. This tiny fishing community became the home of an oyster and crab factory starting in 1926. It was also the birthplace of Supreme Court Justice Clarence Thomas, whose mother worked in the Varn factory and was a crackerjack crab picker with the nickname of Pigeon. She still demonstrates her skills at the museum. Clarence's mother and a lot of others could pick a pound of crab in less than a minute—that's six crabs! And while Pigeon did that, Baby Clarence slept in a crab basket at her feet.

The Varn factory in Pin Point was famous for its deviled crab, a spicy mix that's traditionally stuffed into the empty crab backs, called "barks." The factory lasted right up until 1985, sending its crabmeat and barks and oysters up the coast to restaurants far away.

My absolute favorite local seafood was shrimp, and the sweet little saltwater creek shrimp that can be netted in some places were a special treat. They're the small-fry of the five kinds of shrimp that live in the waters around Savannah, but you can only catch them in the creeks and byways, and the big boats are not allowed to come inland for them. In the old days, they were sold in the streets of Savannah by shrimpers who'd call out, "Swimpee! Fresh swimpee!" If you find some, cook them as simply as possible, in a little butter, just until they turn pink, so you can taste their sweet flavor.

The Southern fish fry is famous for good reason. Partly it's the quality of the fish itself and its freshness, but it's also the frying technique. Look for fish and seafood that's really Southern, caught from North Carolina down through the Gulf Coast. By law there's always a tag to tell you where the seafood was caught, so ask at the market if you don't see it listed. That's how you know you're getting the best in the South. And be sure to read Talking About Frying (page 144) if you're not an old hand at it. There are just a few things to know, but they're important.

out-of-this-world smothered catfish

We ate a lot of catfish when I was growing up, and it was always a good day when we heard somebody had caught some and there'd be a fish fry that night. Daddy's Catfish Stew (page 124) was always the classic at our house, but I've worked out my own version of smothered catfish, and people love this too. The catfish someone caught on a line always seems the tastiest, but whole dressed fish from the market are a close second. **SERVES 6**

1. To make the fish: In a large (5-quart) pot, heat the vegetable oil over medium heat until it registers 375 degrees on a deep-fry thermometer. Have ready a rack set over a baking sheet.

2. Mix the flour, salt, and pepper in a paper bag. One at a time, drop the fish into the paper bag and shake the bag well to cover the fish with flour. Shake excess flour off the fish and put it on a piece of wax paper.

3. When the oil hits the right temperature, fry the catfish, one at a time, until golden brown, giving them 3 minutes on each side. Drain the fish on the rack set over the baking sheet.

4. To make the gravy: Pour off all but ¼ cup of the cooking oil. Over low heat, slowly whisk in the flour, seasoned salt, regular salt, and pepper. Cook, whisking, for about 8 minutes, until the flour and fat mixture reaches a slow boil and has turned a light caramel color. Gradually stir in the water and continue stirring until the gravy has thickened.

5. Add the fish to the gravy, along with the potatoes and peppers. Let simmer for about 12 minutes, until the potato pieces are cooked through.

6. Serve right away, setting one fish over each bowl of hot grits, rice, or brown rice. Ladle on the vegetables and plenty of gravy.

Fish

- 8 cups vegetable oil
- 1 cup self-rising flour
- 1 tablespoon salt
- 1½ teaspoons ground black pepper
- 6 medium dressed catfish (see Tip, page 125; about ½ pound each)

Gravy

- ½ cup all-purpose flour
- 1½ tablespoons Lawry's Seasoned Salt
- ½ tablespoon salt
- ½ teaspoon ground black pepper, or more to taste
- 6 cups water
- 3 medium russet potatoes, peeled and cut into 1-inch pieces
- 1 medium red bell pepper, sliced thin

  Grits, rice, or brown rice, for serving

crab cakes

Crab is expensive, so it's not only a treat, but also something you should take great care with in the cooking. Almost everyone's favorite way with crab is crab cakes, so that's the place to start. Usually big crab cakes are the star of the meal, but it's also fun to make little ones and serve them as appetizers or as party food, stuck with toothpicks on a tray to go with drinks.

You can fry the crab cakes in Crisco, but for a special taste, try them with lard—not the blocks of processed lard in the grocery store, but the rendered lard you find at butcher shops and farmers' markets.

These cakes are so rich and delicious that in a way they're best with just a lemon wedge squeezed over them. But you can add to the glory with a little tartar sauce or rémoulade, which is very traditional in Savannah—though this isn't the classic.

MAKES 8 CRAB CAKES

1. To make the crab cakes: Pour the crab out on a platter and pick it over for bits of shell. Scoop the crab into a large bowl and add all the remaining ingredients. Toss with your hands to combine, trying not to break up the crab. Gently pat the crab into small cakes the size of small burgers (or smaller if you like), handling the crab as little as possible. Put on a plate, cover, and refrigerate for about an hour so the crab cakes won't fall apart in the pan.

2. Put some flour on a saucer and flour the cakes on both sides. Sprinkle a little extra flour on the top and bottom of the cakes and pat it in well.

3. Set the oven to 200 degrees. Melt the Crisco or lard in a large skillet over medium-high heat. The fat should be very hot: Test it by flicking a little flour into the hot fat; it should sizzle and bubble. When it does, slowly ease in the crab cakes, in batches, and cook them until they're golden brown, 6 to 7 minutes on each side. Remove to paper towels to drain, and keep the first batch warm in the oven while you cook the rest.

4. Serve the crab cakes right away with lemon wedges and rémoulade or tartar sauce, if using.

Crab Cakes

- 1 pound fresh lump crabmeat
- 3 green onions (scallions), white and firm green parts, sliced thin (about ½ cup)
- ½ cup finely chopped onion
- ½ cup crushed Ritz crackers
- ½ cup finely chopped green bell pepper
- ¼ cup mayonnaise
- 1 large egg, beaten with a fork
- 1 teaspoon Worcestershire sauce
- 1 teaspoon dry mustard
- ¼ teaspoon granulated garlic
- 1 teaspoon salt
  Dash of cayenne

  Self-rising flour, for dusting
- ½ cup Crisco or lard, for frying
  Lemon wedges, for serving
  Rémoulade Sauce (recipe follows) or Tartar Sauce (page 148), for serving (optional)

rémoulade sauce

MAKES 1 SCANT CUP

1. Combine the vinegar, mustard, ketchup, paprika, salt, and cayenne in a small bowl. Slowly drizzle in the olive oil while whisking constantly. Stir in the green onions.

2. Cover the rémoulade and refrigerate for at least an hour to allow the flavors to develop. It will keep for a week in the refrigerator.

¼ cup tarragon vinegar

2 tablespoons horseradish mustard

1 tablespoon ketchup

1½ teaspoons paprika

½ teaspoon salt

¼ teaspoon cayenne

½ cup extra-virgin olive oil

2 green onions (scallions), white and firm green parts, minced

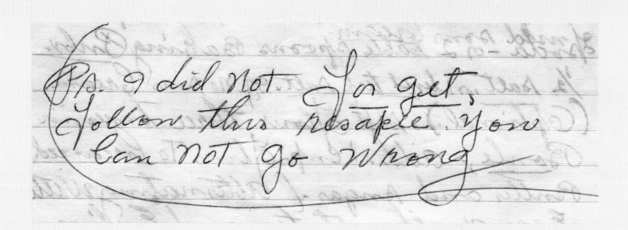

P.S. I did not for get, follow this resaple. You can not go wrong

talking about lard

My grandmother's favorite fats to use were butter, especially home-churned butter from the family cows, and lard, especially lard rendered from their pigs, who rooted around in the yard for acorns and hickory nuts and berries and other treats. She used lard for everything from frying to piecrusts. Later, when she moved from the country to Savannah to take care of her grandchildren after my mother died, she'd use store-bought butter and lard. But when we were told that margarine was supposedly healthier for us, she started using margarine and Crisco more, and butter and lard less.

Now, though, the tide is turning back, and people are starting to realize that butter and lard are actually good for you. The commercial lard that comes in blocks in the grocery store has a lot of additives and is partially hydrogenated so it keeps almost forever. But real rendered lard keeps for a long time too, and it's better because it contains a lot of the same type of good fats as olive oil.

TO MAKE YOUR OWN LARD, the way my grandmother did, look for hard-to-find leaf lard, which comes from around the pig's kidneys and makes the most delicate lard, or unsalted fatback, which comes from the fat just under the back skin. About 3 pounds of fat is a good amount to render.

1. Set the oven to 300 degrees.

2. Cut any skin off the fatback and dice the lard or fatback. Put it in a cast-iron skillet (you'll be seasoning the pan at the same time) or a roasting pan, add ⅓ cup water for each pound of fat, and stir. Slide the skillet into the oven and leave it there for about 3 hours, stirring every half hour. The fat will slowly render out, the water will disappear, and you'll be left with liquid gold and some delicious crunchy cracklings, which will sink to the bottom of the skillet when the lard has nearly finished cooking. Scoop them out and serve them as a snack.

3. Filter the liquid lard through several layers of cheesecloth into several jars or into muffin tins. Once the lard cools, the fat will turn white and solid. Lard in sealed jars will keep in the refrigerator for at least 6 months. Or store muffin-shaped lard blocks in a zipper-lock bag in the freezer for well over a year.

crab casserole

My sister Marilyn is a great cook who's well known for her crab dishes. This one is a favorite. In the Lowcountry, any "casserole" that has to do with seafood isn't something in a creamy sauce baked in a big ovenproof dish. It's a smaller, intensely flavored baked concoction from which you take small helpings. Usually the only starch involved is crackers, and here it's our old friend Ritz.

SERVES 6 AS AN APPETIZER OR PART OF A BUFFET

1. Set the oven to 350 degrees. Lightly butter an 8-x-8-x-2-inch baking dish.

2. Mix all the ingredients together gently and spoon into the baking dish. Bake, uncovered, for 1 hour. Let sit for at least 5 minutes before serving.

3. Serve warm or at room temperature.

1 pound fresh lump crabmeat, picked over for bits of shell

1 sleeve Ritz crackers (about 26), crumbled

1 medium onion, diced

⅓ cup each chopped green and red bell pepper

1 large egg, beaten with a fork

3 tablespoons mayonnaise

1 tablespoon Worcestershire sauce

1 teaspoon crushed red pepper

½ teaspoon granulated garlic

¼ teaspoon ground black pepper

talking about frying

We Southerners love fried food so much that it's almost a joke in other parts of the country. But if you know what you're doing, as most of us do, it's not only easy and delicious, it's also not unhealthy, because the food should absorb almost none of the fat. There are just a few things to remember.

the basics

DEEP-FRYING

You'll need either an electric fryer or a deep heavy pot, like a Dutch oven. If you have the space for it, a deep fryer will make frying an almost foolproof pleasure.

Follow the instructions for the electric fryer when you fill it with oil. For a Dutch oven, add the frying fat to the pot so it's anywhere from 3 to 4 inches deep—but never fill the pot more than halfway. It's a good idea to measure water into the pot to see how much it takes to get 4 inches in the pot, so you can just measure the fat when you're ready to fry. (Just be sure you dry the pot well before you fill it with fat!)

Many deep fryers come with glass lids so you can see what's going on and vents for the steam, so the food stays crisp. My favorite is a double fryer; Fingerhut has one with a divider and separate controls for the two separate frying wells so I can fry fish and hushpuppies at the same time.

THE FAT

A good frying fat is stable and won't break down easily. Any of the ones listed here will work fine:

- **Crisco:** the modern favorite, highly processed to be stable, this produces a sweet flavor and crisp results.
- **Rendered lard from a butcher or farmers' market:** the classic, used for well over two centuries, this extremely stable natural fat has a delicious flavor and produces crisp fried food. My grandmother's favorite. Supermarket lard doesn't have much flavor, but it will work for frying.
- **Vegetable oil:** highly processed, very stable, flavorless.
- **Peanut oil:** quite stable, with a subtle nutty flavor.
- **Bacon grease:** very stable, with the great flavor of bacon, which seems to go with everything. You can add just a little bacon grease to perk up flavorless oils, which don't contribute much to the party.
- **Light olive oil:** has been stabilized, so you can fry with it. You get some of the healthy qualities of virgin oils without all the flavor.

tools

DEEP-FRY THERMOMETER

You'll want a deep-fry thermometer to keep the temperature at a steady level. Choose one that's easy to read; in all the chaos of frying, you don't want to be sticking your face near the bubbling oil to try to read the temperature. For deep-frying, it should be 365 or 375 degrees; generally the closer you keep the temperature to 375 degrees, the less oil goes into the food.

SPATTER GUARD

Inexperienced fry cooks can make quite a mess, so save yourself some grief with a sturdy spatter guard that can go in the dishwasher.

DRAINING RACK

Set a baking rack over a cookie sheet for draining just-fried foods. You can use up a lot of paper towels draining fried food and some experts say draining on paper towels actually lets some of the frying fat soak back into the food. The rack-and-sheet method works perfectly, and if you put a folded-up paper bag (it can be the same bag you used to flour the food) under the rack, you can just toss out the oily paper bag when you're done.

tips

- Corn flour is the finest grade of cornmeal and it makes a great coating for fried fish and other foods. If you don't see it at the market or just need some right this minute, grind up some cornmeal in a food processor or blender.
- Self-rising flour will give you the crispest crust on your fried food. To make your own, see page 75.
- Add foods to the hot fat slowly, one edge at a time for larger pieces. A lot of food going in at once can splash fat out of the pan dangerously and lower the temperature so the food gets soggy. The fat will bubble up in small bubbles around the food at the right temperature.
- If you're frying in batches, be sure to scoop out any coating that's fallen to the bottom of the pot with a slotted spoon—if you don't, it could burn and ruin the flavor of the next batches.
- Always keep your eyes on frying food because the hot fat can boil over in a moment and start a fire (douse it with salt or baking soda). Ideally you want to have 3 inches of space above the frying food in the pot, so be sure the fat doesn't come more than halfway up the sides of the pot. A third of the way up is even safer.
- If you have an accident and some hot grease gets on your skin, put the burn under cold running water immediately and let it take the heat out. Then put some yellow mustard on the burn—a tip from the People's Pharmacy that really works. Just leave it on until you're ready for bed, then rinse it off and dry the burn carefully by patting it very gently with a very clean towel.

buttermilk-battered panfried fish fillets

A little buttermilk bath does wonders for fresh fish fillets such as catfish, flounder, trout, or grouper. Just half an hour in the buttermilk will sweeten the fish and keep it deliciously moist. In the old days, we'd fry the fish in Crisco, but now it's usually vegetable oil, with maybe a little bacon grease or butter for flavor.

You have some options for the coating: self-rising flour with a little extra salt and pepper and a pinch of cayenne is classic, as is cornmeal mixed with salt and pepper. But you can even use Bisquick mix plus a little salt and cayenne.

It's traditional to serve hushpuppies (page 87) with the fish, along with tartar sauce and some lemon wedges to squeeze over the fish. Fried catfish also makes a great sandwich on a bun, with some shredded lettuce and rémoulade sauce (page 141). **SERVES 4**

1. Pour some of the buttermilk into a shallow baking dish and add the fish fillets; add more buttermilk as needed to completely cover all the fillets. Let them rest for half an hour.

2. Set the oven for 200 degrees to keep the first batch of fish hot. Warm a serving platter in the oven. Have ready a baking rack set on top of a baking sheet for draining the fish.

3. Put the seasoned flour (or cornmeal or Bisquick) on a plate or a small platter. One at a time, shake any extra buttermilk off each fillet and dip it into the flour on both sides, being sure it is covered, but not too thickly, then shake off any extra flour and lay the fillets on wax paper.

4. Heat a heavy skillet at least 10 inches wide over medium-high heat. When it's hot, add the oil or lard to a depth of ¼ inch, then add the bacon grease or butter. When the fat is sizzling, drop in half the fish. Fry until crisp and golden on the bottom, about 3 minutes, or longer for thicker fillets, then turn the pieces—just once!—with a long wide spatula and let crisp on the bottom. Drain on the rack and keep warm—still on the

1 quart buttermilk

1⅓ pounds fresh fish fillets (catfish, flounder, trout, or grouper; see Tips), cut into serving pieces

1 cup self-rising flour, seasoned with salt, pepper, and a pinch of cayenne

or

1 cup cornmeal or corn flour (see Tips, page 145), seasoned with salt, pepper, and cayenne

or

1 cup Bisquick, lumps pressed out with a fork and seasoned with salt and cayenne

1 scant cup vegetable oil, peanut oil, or lard, or more as needed (see Tips)

1 tablespoon bacon grease or butter

Lemon wedges and tartar sauce, homemade (recipe follows) or store-bought, for serving

rack—in the oven until all the fish is cooked. Add more oil or lard to the pan if needed to fry the second batch, and make sure it's hot before adding the fish.

5. Serve on a platter surrounded with lemon wedges, with tartar sauce on the side.

TIPS

• If you're going to make hushpuppies (page 87) in the same skillet (like I do), use 1½ inches oil to fry the fish. When the fish are done, keep them warm in a 200-degree oven and the fat hot in the pan to fry the hushpuppies.

• You can also deep-fry the fillets in a 12-inch skillet, which makes sense if you're frying a lot of fish: You'll need 3 inches of oil or lard (but don't fill the skillet more than half full). For more frying tips, read Talking About Frying (page 144).

• If you're going to be cooking a lot of fried fish, or fried food in general, it's worth getting a deep fryer.

---

homemade tartar sauce

MAKES ABOUT 1⅓ CUPS

Stir everything except the cayenne or mustard together in a small bowl. Let it sit for a bit to mellow and then taste it—you may want to add more lemon juice or some cayenne or Dijon mustard.

1 cup mayonnaise

¼ cup finely chopped dill pickles or sweet pickle relish

2 green onions (scallions), white and firm green parts, minced

1 tablespoon snipped fresh dill

Fresh lemon juice to taste (start with 2 teaspoons)

Salt and ground black pepper to taste

Cayenne or Dijon mustard (optional)

"barbecued" shrimp

You don't actually cook this shrimp on the grill, you broil it—and it makes the greatest tangy, buttery, and lemony sauce while it cooks. The shrimp are cooked and served in the shells, which keeps them succulent and moderates the effect of the spices. This is a communal feast, with everyone dipping bread into the sauce in the baking dish. It may seem like there's too much butter on the shrimp, but remember that you're serving this with lots of crusty French bread, and all that sauce will disappear—don't worry. A little dirty rice (page 71) on the side is also a great idea.

SERVES 6

1. Heat the broiler to high and set a rack in the oven so it's 6 or 7 inches away from the heat.

2. Arrange the shrimp in a flameproof baking dish large enough to hold all of them in one layer. Drizzle olive oil over them and turn them over in the oil. Cover the shrimp thickly with the black pepper; more is better. Add salt generously, then add the garlic, Worcestershire sauce, lemon juice, several jolts of hot sauce, and the Creole seasoning. Arrange the butter slices over the top of the shrimp and tuck the lemon slices in around them.

3. Broil until the shrimp are just cooked through, about 10 minutes. They should be pink and firm to the touch. Taste one to be sure they're cooked.

4. Serve in the baking dish with French bread and a lot of napkins for the shrimp peelers.

1½ pounds shell-on jumbo or large shrimp

Extra-virgin olive oil, for drizzling

1 tablespoon cracked or coarsely ground black pepper, or more to taste

Salt to taste

2 garlic cloves, minced

⅓ cup Worcestershire sauce

3 lemons: 2 juiced, 1 sliced thin

Hot sauce (Texas Pete or Tabasco)

2 teaspoons Creole seasoning, such as Emeril's (see Tip)

2 sticks (½ pound) butter, sliced

1 large loaf French bread, for serving

TIP

No one bothers to devein barbecued shrimp. If you want to, cut down the back of the shrimp with kitchen scissors, leaving the shell, along with the tail, on. Pull out the vein. If you're using frozen shrimp, you can buy it deveined.

TIP

If you don't have Creole seasoning, use 1 teaspoon paprika and ½ teaspoon each dried oregano and dried thyme.

shrimp gumbo

My gumbo recipe isn't like most others. I don't like to stand over the stove stirring the roux forever before I can even start making the gumbo. Instead, I stir in a little flour and water at the end of the cooking. This is a lighter version, one that's not as thick or gloppy as the old New Orleans–style gumbo.

Serve the gumbo over brown or white rice. **SERVES 4 TO 6**

1. In a 2-quart saucepan, sauté the celery and onion in the oil over medium heat until the onion is translucent, about 5 minutes. Add all the remaining ingredients except the shrimp, flour, and water (and rice), cover the pan, and simmer gently for 30 minutes.

2. Add the shrimp, cover, and cook for 15 minutes.

3. In a small bowl, mix the flour with the water and add slowly to the gumbo. You may not need to add it all, so add a little, stir the gumbo for a few minutes, and see how thick it gets. You don't want this gumbo too thick; it should be more soupy than stewy.

4. Remove the bay leaves and serve in shallow soup bowls, over rice if you like.

- 1 cup chopped celery
- 1 cup chopped onion
- 1 tablespoon extra-virgin olive oil
- 1 (14.5-ounce) can petite diced tomatoes
- 1 cup 1-inch pieces trimmed fresh okra or frozen cut-up okra
- 2 bay leaves
- 1 teaspoon lemon pepper seasoning
- ½ teaspoon dried thyme
- 1½ teaspoons Dora's Savannah Seasoning (page 79)
- 1 chicken bouillon cube
- 1 cup chicken stock
- 1½ pounds small shrimp, peeled and deveined
- 1 tablespoon all-purpose flour
- 2 tablespoons water
- Foolproof Rice, for serving (page 220; optional)

TIP

You can substitute larger shrimp, about 2 pounds, to make this dish more elegant.

MURALS

The murals on the factory walls were painted in the mid-1990s by Sharon Varn, the wife of Algernon S. Varn III, as a tribute to the people of Pin Point. The scenes depict daily life at the factory, including men working, women drawing water and children playing. The legendary fisherman John Henry Haynes, better known as "Bacon," requested that his name be painted above his image after he passed away. The murals have been the subject of numerous professional photographers and have been recognized by the Beach Institute, which displays African-American art in Savannah.

PICKING & COOLING HOUSE

jambalaya

I've heard it said that jambalaya is just Savannah Red Rice (page 173) with several kinds of meat and shrimp in it. That's sort of true, though they might give you an argument about that in Louisiana, where it originated. This is a really useful recipe—you can add leftovers as you like and expand it to serve more people if you need to, and it's one of those dishes that's easy to put together. **SERVES 10**

1. Set the oven to 350 degrees.

2. In a Dutch oven, fry the bacon pieces over medium heat just until browned—you don't want them to get crisp. Drain the bacon on paper towels. Brown the kielbasa chunks in the bacon fat, then scoop them out and set aside.

3. Add the green peppers, celery, onion, garlic, jalapeño, and thyme to the fat in the pot and cook over medium heat, stirring almost constantly, until the vegetables are softened, about 5 minutes. Stir in the tomato paste. Add the rice and stir until the rice turns white.

4. Return the bacon and kielbasa to the pot. Add the tomatoes and chicken stock and season with salt and pepper to taste, stirring well. Bring the liquid to a boil, cover the pot, put in the oven, and bake for 25 minutes.

5. Remove the pot from the oven and add the shrimp, tucking them into the bed of rice. Put the pot back in the oven and bake until the stock has been absorbed and the rice is tender and moist, 20 to 25 minutes.

6. Serve right away, or let sit for up to an hour (see Tip).

½ pound bacon strips, cut into 1-inch slices

1 pound kielbasa, cut into ½-inch chunks

2 medium green bell peppers, chopped

2 celery ribs, chopped

1 large onion, chopped

3 garlic cloves, minced

1 jalapeño, minced

1 teaspoon dried thyme

2 tablespoons tomato paste

2 cups long-grain white rice or Converted (parboiled) rice, rinsed

1 (28-ounce) can diced fire-roasted tomatoes, with their juice

3 cups chicken stock

Salt and ground black pepper to taste

1½ pounds medium shrimp, peeled and deveined

> **TIP**
>
> You can substitute smoked ham for the kielbasa or add cut-up leftover chicken.

> **TIP**
>
> If you're taking this dish to a potluck, cover it in its pot, and it will still be warm and delicious an hour later.

roasted shrimp with cherry tomatoes and pasta

This colorful dish is simple and yet it has so many flavors that all come together beautifully. It may even remind you a little of shrimp and grits. My secret ingredient is bacon—that's what sets it apart from all the other versions of this dish. You can play with it depending on what you have in the kitchen. It's really good with any kind of skinny pasta, like spaghetti or even linguine, but you can make it with grits or rice too.

Don't pass this recipe by just because you don't have any sage. If you have fresh basil, tear up the same amount of leaves but don't add them until the dish goes together, so they don't shrivel up and turn black in the oven. If you only have dried herbs, try a sprinkle of oregano over the raw shrimp.

With a green salad and maybe some garlic bread, this makes a light supper that can even work for company.   **SERVES 6**

1. Set the oven to 350 degrees. Adjust the rack positions to the middle and top third.

2. Put a very large pot of water on to boil for cooking the pasta.

3. Place the shrimp in a single layer on one side of a baking sheet; scatter the bacon pieces over the other side. Drizzle a little olive oil over the shrimp, so they can hold the seasoning. Sprinkle salt and pepper over the shrimp and arrange the fresh sage leaves on top.

4. Put the cherry tomatoes and bell pepper strips in a bowl, drizzle with olive oil, and toss. Add salt and pepper and toss again. Spread the vegetables on another baking sheet.

5. Put the vegetables on the middle oven rack and roast until the tomatoes burst and the pepper strips are tender, 10 to 15 minutes. Meantime, put the shrimp and bacon on the top rack and roast until the shrimp are cooked through—they'll

1½ pounds large shrimp, peeled and deveined

6 bacon slices, cut into ½-inch-wide pieces

Up to ⅓ cup extra-virgin olive oil, for drizzling

Salt and cracked black pepper to taste

10 fresh sage leaves

12 each red and yellow cherry tomatoes

½ orange or red bell pepper, sliced thin

1 pound angel hair pasta or linguine

1½ tablespoons red wine vinegar

be pink and curled into little C shapes—and the bacon is browned, 10 to 12 minutes.

6. Check the cooking time for the pasta if you're not making angel hair—you want it to be cooked and drained just after the shrimp, bacon, and vegetables are done.

7. Just before it's all ready, a few minutes for angel hair or about 12 minutes for linguine, add salt to the boiling water, add the pasta, and boil until it's just tender. Drain immediately and dump it into a large serving bowl. Add a spoonful of olive oil and toss well.

8. Add the shrimp, tomatoes, bacon, and any drippings to the pasta, then add the red wine vinegar and toss. Add a bit more olive oil if you like. Serve immediately.

TIPS

• Bacon will slice best when it's just out of the refrigerator.

• To minimize cleanup, you can line the baking sheets with foil or parchment paper.

sunday picnics
and church suppers

WHEN I WAS GROWING UP IN SAVANNAH, we loved to go to the beach on
Hilton Head with a big picnic lunch. No blacks were allowed on the beach at
Tybee Island, just off Savannah, but there were two beaches right next to each
other on Hilton Head and you could wander over them as you liked. They were
beautiful, and we'd settle in for the day with our fried chicken and sandwiches
and bottles of grape or orange Nehi or RC to wash it all down. We always had
some parched peanuts to drop down into our pop bottles once we'd drunk
about half of it, and the peanuts would make it bubble up and get all fizzy.

Later on, the beaches at Tybee opened up for us, and that's much closer than
Hilton Head, so we'd go there, maybe stopping for some boiled peanuts on the
way. Now that beautiful long double beach on Hilton Head is all private and
fenced off so no one can go there.

Our other favorite picnic area was Hutchinson Island in the river right off
Savannah. You could hire a boat to take you there and stay for a few hours
before it would bring you back. One part of the island was owned by black
people, and they had a lot of food stands and music pavilions, and you could
wander from one food place to another getting your lunch or dinner together.
Once you had your barbecue or fish fry and your corn or shrimp or Lowcountry
boil or whatever else you wanted, you'd eat it on the grass, listening to the
music and watching all the happy people enjoying themselves. At night it was

club time and there were lights strung in the trees, and you'd dance the night away. It was all a big glorious party, like a day in the country with great food.

We still love our picnics, but now that Hutchinson has been developed and the party is over, we picnic right in the middle of Savannah at Forsyth Park, near the famous fountain. I gather my daughter and my four grandsons and others in the family who can come, and we have the same great food and good times we always did.

Summer picnics after church on Sunday always seem like such a good idea, but for the first nineteen of the twenty-two years I was working with Paula Deen, Sundays were workdays, so there was no church and no picnics for me. I'm a big Church Lady, so I really missed it. My church is small, and my extended family is large, so when we all go, we take up at least half the pews. I've got Sundays free now, so I often bake something to bring for everyone after church. Once you make something everyone goes crazy for, though, like my Banana Pudding (page 239), you've got to keep bringing it, or you'll see a lot of sad faces.

I don't know if church homecomings happen outside the South, but if you get a chance to go to one, go! These events, usually held in the summer and also sometimes around the winter holidays, welcome back everyone who's ever gone to that church, and their friends, and anyone else who wants to come. Often they're advertised in the local newspaper and total strangers are welcome. There's a church service that focuses on the families who've come home, and then every-one wanders over to the church hall or the lawn where tables are set up and an eye-popping potluck church supper awaits.

You'll see seas of casseroles, mounds of fried chicken, roasts, hams, dozens of salads, pots and pots of baked beans, hundreds of cheerful deviled eggs, and dish-es you might not even recognize—all homemade by different hands. Everyone eats too much, because you just have to taste everything—and when it's slap yo' mama good, you have to have a little more.

The most amazing homecoming I know about happens at my friend Felicia's church in Savannah just before Christmas, on the third Sunday in December. It's a big church, and people come from all over—Felicia's family comes back for Christ-mas from Florida, Chicago, Indiana, and points west, and homecoming is their first sight of all their old friends and whole family. This church had a homecoming long before they had a church hall, and they held it in the parking lot. The food

was served from the open trunks of the cars, with all pies in one car, all cakes in another, and hams and fried chicken in another, so people could wander from car to car and fill their plates.

Now that they have the church hall, it's an even bigger feast, and lately they've started cooking up a Lowcountry boil with crabs and corn in a giant pot outside in back of the church hall. They also fry fish in huge outdoor fryers, and frying biscuits too. You'd think that people would make a beeline for the best cooks' famous dishes, but Felicia says it's not like that, because what you bring, you bring to share. There's a good family feeling that extends to the food, and no one takes a proud attitude: Everyone appreciates it all. They keep to the old idea of having all the meats together, all the starches in one area, all the desserts in another, for dozens and dozens of kinds of foods. I love the idea of homecoming, and I know what it would have meant to me in my years of exile in Pennsylvania to be able to come home to an event like that at Christmas.

The dishes in this chapter travel well, of course, because they have to go on the road, but they're just as good for a little homecoming at your house.

tomato sandwich

Nothing says summer like a Southern tomato sandwich. The most basic version is just sliced white bread slathered with Duke's mayonnaise and piled with salted sliced dead-ripe tomatoes. I have my own version, which doesn't get all sogged out with leaking tomato juice when you take it on a picnic.

If you have a craving, you can make a tomato sandwich in winter with supermarket hothouse tomatoes, the ones called Camparis that come with stems on and actually smell like tomatoes. It's not the same, but it's pretty good.

MAKES 1 SANDWICH

1. Start about an hour before you want to put the sandwich together so you have time to drain the tomatoes. Put the tomato slices on paper towels to drain for an hour, turning them once after ½ hour.

2. Meantime, mix the mayonnaise with the Savannah seasoning—start with just a pinch and work your way up to a taste you like.

3. When the tomatoes are drained, smear both the top and bottom slices of the bread with the seasoned mayonnaise and arrange the drained tomato slices in between. Wrap well in wax paper for a picnic or slice diagonally in half and serve right away.

1 vine-ripe tomato, sliced medium thick

1 tablespoon Duke's mayonnaise or Miracle Whip, or more if you like

Dora's Savannah Seasoning (page 79)

2 slices fine-textured white bread

deviled eggs

I don't think I've ever seen leftover deviled eggs. However many there are, they all seem to be eaten up, and often they're the first thing to go. Plain deviled eggs are just great, so don't feel like you have to make them fancy. But if you do want to dress them up, you can add cooked shrimp or bacon (recipes follow), or you could just add 3 tablespoons cooked crabmeat to the egg yolks. A little paprika dust on top does wonders for any filling.

If the stuffed eggs are traveling, the easiest way to carry them is to arrange them on a deviled egg plate—the ones with egg-shaped hollows. That way, they won't slip and slide all over the place. Look for older ones at yard sales.

MAKES 12 STUFFED EGGS

1. Peel the cooked eggs and slice them lengthwise in half. With a spoon, scoop the yolks out into a small bowl. Mash the egg yolks with a fork and then mix in all the remaining ingredients except the paprika. The mixture should be smooth and creamy. Taste and correct the seasoning if necessary.

2. Stuff each egg white half with about ¾ tablespoon of the yolk mixture. Dust the finished eggs with paprika.

3. Cover the eggs loosely with plastic wrap and refrigerate if you're not serving right away.

6 large hard-boiled eggs (see Box, page 165)

3 tablespoons mayonnaise or Miracle Whip

½ teaspoon yellow mustard

Accent to taste (optional)

1 shake Texas Pete or other hot sauce

½ teaspoon salt, or more to taste

¼ teaspoon black pepper, or more to taste

2 tablespoons sweet pickle relish

Paprika, for dusting

sailboat eggs

These simple deviled eggs look and taste just great with a little piece of Scrumptious Bacon (page 55) stuck into the yellow filling. Cut the bacon into 1-inch pieces, then into triangles. Stick them in the filling to make little sails.

continued...

> **TIP**
>
> If you're serving deviled eggs on a regular platter, cut a small slice off the curved bottom of each egg white so they can sit flat on their butts.

deviled eggs with shrimp

While the eggs are cooking, put a medium saucepan of water with a big pinch of Old Bay Seasoning on to boil. Taste the water once it's boiling—it may need more seasoning to be flavorful. Toss in 6 medium peeled and deveined shrimp, cover the pan, turn off the heat, and let stand for 10 minutes, or until the shrimp are pink and cooked through. Drain and let cool.

Mince the shrimp and add them to the egg yolk mixture along with ⅛ teaspoon Old Bay Seasoning. Top the finished deviled eggs with snipped fresh dill.

deviled eggs with bacon

While the eggs are cooking, fry 2 slices of bacon. Drain on paper towels and then crumble the bacon into the egg yolk mixture. Top the finished eggs with a dusting of paprika.

cracking the hard-boiled egg code

I cook my hard-boiled eggs for 20 minutes, which is longer than you may do it. I don't want them to be even a tiny bit runny in the yolk, and 20 minutes will do it without making any gray rings around the yellow. And I never have a problem peeling my eggs.

Here's how I do it: Put the eggs in a saucepan in a single layer and cover well with cold water. If you're boiling really fresh eggs, put a teaspoon of baking soda in the cooking water along with the eggs, which will loosen the tight grip of the white membrane that separates each egg from its shell and make it easier to peel. Bring the eggs to a boil, then cook uncovered at a gentle boil for 20 minutes. Put the eggs into cold water right away and crack both ends, then crack the eggs all over. Put them back in the cold water until they cool down a bit.

When the eggs are no longer hot, peel them—this will be easy with older eggs. Just-laid eggs are a little harder.

boiled peanuts

My grandmother used to make boiled peanuts in the country with her family's freshly dug peanut harvest. That's what you need for great boiled peanuts. They're called "green peanuts," and they're available for only a short time and have to be kept cold. In southern Georgia, the harvest is from August until the first of October. You'll probably have to mail-order green peanuts in season (see Sources, page 263). They couldn't be easier to cook. You can boil a bunch of them, then freeze them in smaller packets and have boiled peanuts all year long.

The story goes that the original boiled peanuts were cooked in seawater, which is a great idea. Even better if you throw in a few tablespoonfuls of Old Bay Seasoning.

MAKES 5 POUNDS

1. Rinse the peanuts well and pinch off their little tips, so more of the brine will get inside the shells and they'll be easier to crack.

2. Fill a large pot with the water. Add the peanuts and the salt or Old Bay and stir well. Bring the water to a boil, then simmer over medium heat, uncovered, for about 1½ hours (or longer if the peanuts are still not soft), giving the pot a stir every now and then and replacing the water as needed with more hot water. Some of the peanuts may float at first—don't worry about that, they'll control themselves later. Check every 20 minutes or so after the first 45 minutes, to see if the peanuts are done. They should be soft but still have a little firmness; you don't want them to be mushy.

3. Once the peanuts are ready, if they seem too salty, pour off the water, replace it with fresh cool water, and let the peanuts sit in it and lose salt as they cool down. Once they're cool, drain them.

4. Serve the peanuts warm, reheated in a microwave oven, or at room temperature. They'll keep about a week, covered, in the refrigerator. Or freeze them in plastic bags and thaw before serving or reheating.

5 pounds green peanuts in the shell (see Sources, page 263)

4 quarts water or seawater

⅔ cup salt, if you're using tap water

3 tablespoons Old Bay Seasoning, if you're using seawater

parched peanuts

Parched (roasted in the shell) peanuts are even easier to make than boiled, and you don't have to use the freshest peanuts, though you may have to adjust the cooking time depending on how old your peanuts are. Some peanuts can be well over a year old when you buy them. **MAKES 2 POUNDS**

1. Set the oven to 350 degrees.

2. Scatter the peanuts in a single layer on one or two baking sheets. Roast for 20 minutes. Remove a couple and let cool, then taste. If they don't taste roasted, keep checking them every 3 minutes until they taste right. Sprinkle salt over the peanuts and let them cool a bit before serving them—they are *hot.* Serve warm or at room temperature.

3. Store tightly sealed at room temperature for up to 10 days.

2 pounds raw peanuts in the shell

Salt to taste

hot goobers
the boiled and the parched

Georgia is one of the big home states of the humble peanut, and we are just crazy for them. Blister-fried, plain old roasted in the shells (which we call "parched" in our part of the South), or boiled, we love them all.

If you've never had a boiled (some people say "bald") peanut, you really ought to try some. Some fans even eat the smaller boiled peanut shells along with slurping up the brine inside the shells.

If you're driving around the Lowcountry, it won't take you long to come across someone selling boiled peanuts on the side of the road, usually with a big kettle or an old tin washtub of them steaming away in their brine. In Savannah, Daddy used to go to his favorite peanut connection, a black man who had fixed up his bike to have a hot box on it for boiled peanuts. He was always on West Broad Street, now Martin Luther King Boulevard.

Peanuts in the shell, boiled or parched, are ready to go with you, just right for a picnic or the beach run, or anywhere outdoors, where the shells won't make a big mess. They're great for school lunches or after-school munchies, and they're a healthy snack.

baked spaghetti

Spaghetti with meat sauce is wonderful on its own, of course, but when you layer it in a casserole, giving it a kind of lasagna treatment, the flavors go all through the dish and deepen into something different. The dish is also very convenient—you can have it standing by in the freezer or the refrigerator, just waiting to be baked or reheated. And it's easily carried away to someone else's house for a potluck.

SERVES 6 TO 8

1. Combine the tomato sauce, tomatoes and their juice, all the vegetables, the herbs, butter, sugar, bouillon cubes, sherry, Worcestershire, and most of the Savannah seasoning in a large pot. Stir well to mix everything and bring to a boil, then reduce the heat and simmer, covered, for 1½ hours, stirring regularly so nothing sticks.

2. Meantime, add the beef and the rest of the Savannah seasoning to a skillet or large saucepan and cook, stirring, over medium-high heat until the meat's crumbled and lightly browned, about 10 minutes. Drain the fat and set aside.

3. Add the cooked beef to the pot with the sauce and simmer, stirring occasionally, for another 30 minutes.

4. While the sauce simmers, bring a large pot of salted water to a boil and cook the pasta according to the package directions until it's tender-firm. Rinse and drain it.

5. Mix together the two cheeses.

6. Set the oven to 350 degrees. Spray or brush the bottom of a 9-x-13-x-2-inch casserole dish with olive oil.

7. Add a little sauce to the bottom of the dish. Add a layer of pasta, then more sauce, then ½ cup of the combined cheeses. Top with another layer of pasta, then sauce, and then cheese. Repeat, making 2 layers of pasta, sauce, and cheese, ending

- 3 cups jarred or canned tomato sauce
- 2 cups canned diced tomatoes, with their juice
- ½ cup diced onion
- ½ cup diced green bell pepper
- ½ cup diced celery
- 2 garlic cloves, chopped
- ¼ cup chopped fresh parsley
- 1½ teaspoons Italian seasoning
- 1 teaspoon dried oregano
- 2 bay leaves
- 1 tablespoon butter
- 2 teaspoons sugar
- 2 beef bouillon cubes
- 1 tablespoon sherry
- 1 tablespoon Worcestershire sauce
- 1½ teaspoons Dora's Savannah Seasoning (page 79)
- 1½ pounds ground beef
- ½ pound spaghetti
- 1½ cups shredded cheddar cheese
- 1½ cups shredded Monterey Jack cheese
- Olive oil, for the casserole dish

with sauce. You will have a small amount of cheese left,
½ cup or more. Set aside.

8. Put the casserole dish in the oven, with a baking sheet
under it just in case it bubbles over, and bake until it's heated
through, about 30 minutes.

9. Take out the casserole and top with the remaining cheese,
then put the casserole back in the oven just until the cheese on
top is thoroughly melted and bubbling. Serve hot.

fried chicken salad

Whether I'm making homemade fried chicken or ordering takeout, I never worry about having too much, because if you don't polish it all off at once, the leftovers will make a tasty salad the next day. You can also make this salad on the fly by picking up some freshly cooked fried chicken tenders at the market.

Here's how to make the salad: Before you refrigerate your leftover fried chicken, pull the meat from the bones and cut it into small slices. Put them in a bowl. Include any bits of coating that fall off. (If you're using fried cutlets or tenders, just slice them up.) Add some sliced green onions (scallions), chopped fresh parsley, and chopped small inner ribs of celery, including some of the pale leaves. If you have some fresh dill, that's also good in the salad. Toasted slivered almonds are nice too for some crunch.

For the dressing, mix together some mayonnaise and fresh lemon juice to taste in a small bowl. Add a pressed or minced garlic clove and mix in well. You can include a little finely grated lemon zest too. Add the dressing to the bowl of chicken, toss everything together, and taste for salt and pepper. Let the salad sit at room temperature a little, and serve it on a platter over fresh greens—such as baby spinach or thin-sliced romaine.

three-cheese mac 'n' cheese with sour cream

This dish turns up, *must* turn up, on almost every Southern feast table, even at Christmas. You can't serve ham without it, but it can also be dinner all by itself, with a salad or some good sliced tomatoes on the side. My version is very creamy and also very easy. You don't have to make a sauce, but you do have to watch a couple of points in the process. These are clear in the directions, and they're not fatal mistakes. But to get a really creamy, thick sauce with just the right seasoning, they're good tricks to know. **SERVES 6 TO 8**

1. Set the oven to 350 degrees. Butter a 9-x-13-inch casserole dish.

2. Set a large pot of water on to boil. When it boils, add a little salt and then the macaroni. You want the noodles to cook until they're just soft all the way through, as though you were making a macaroni salad—firm-soft. If you overcook them and they're all floppy, it's not the end of the world, but the dish won't be quite as good. When the noodles are firm-soft, dump them into a colander in the sink and drain thoroughly.

3. Put the macaroni in a large bowl and stir in the cheddar cheese. Mix well, then stir in half the mozzarella and Jack mixture. Stir well, add the sour cream, and mix well again. Stir in 1 cup of the milk—if the noodles are a little undercooked, they'll gobble up most of the milk and you'll need to add more.

4. Add salt and pepper to taste, starting with about 1 teaspoon salt. It's okay if it tastes a little salty—when the eggs go in, they'll temper any extra saltiness. Stir in the eggs.

5. Pour the macaroni into the casserole dish and scatter the remaining 1 cup mozzarella/Jack over the top. Bake until the casserole is bubbling and the cheese on top is golden brown, 20 to 30 minutes. Serve hot or warm.

Salt

1 pound elbow macaroni

2 cups shredded sharp cheddar cheese

2 cups mixed shredded mozzarella and Monterey Jack cheese

1 (8-ounce) container sour cream

1–1½ cups milk, as needed

Ground black pepper to taste

4 large eggs, beaten well with a fork

oven-baked savannah red rice

Red rice is a signature dish in Savannah, so it better be good. I used to have a problem cooking red rice on top of the stove. It would always sog out on me, and I hated that. Finally it dawned on me that it might work better baked in the oven, and I was so happy the first time I tried it that way. Now it's one of my favorite dishes.

First you make a delicious sauce that cooks down a bit, then you layer rice, sauce, vegetables, and butter in the baking dish. It all bakes together, and I give you my word, it's never soggy.

This recipe uses turkey sausage, which makes the dish a little lighter, but you could use another kind of smoky sausage if you'd rather. The only other remarkable ingredient is Texas Pete, a great hot sauce featuring three different peppers, which is not actually from Texas but from North Carolina. **SERVES 25 TO 30**

1. In an 8-quart pot, combine the tomato sauce and diced tomatoes (put both cans aside to measure the water), tomato paste, bacon (or frying grease or oil), hot sauce, sausage, Savannah seasoning, sugar, and Accent (if using). Fill the tomato sauce and diced tomato cans with water, add it to the pot, and stir well. Cook over medium heat, uncovered, for 45 minutes, stirring from time to time.

2. Toward the end of the cooking time, set the oven to 350 degrees.

3. Pour the rice into an 8-quart (20-x-12-inch) baking dish or divide it between two 9-x-12-inch baking dishes. Spread the rice out evenly. Measure out 9 cups of the tomato sauce and spread it over the rice; save the remaining sauce for later. Scatter the peppers and onions over the tomato sauce. Cut the butter into small pieces and scatter it over the top.

4. Cover the dish with a lid or seal it tightly with foil and bake for 45 minutes.

1 (28-ounce) can tomato sauce

1 (28-ounce) can petite diced tomatoes

1 (6-ounce) can tomato paste

1 cup bacon grease (if you have it) or fry-meat grease (see page 68) or vegetable oil

¼ cup Texas Pete or other hot sauce

4 cups sliced smoked sausage (about 2 pounds), such as Hillshire Farms smoked turkey sausage or kielbasa

3 tablespoons Dora's Savannah Seasoning (page 79)

3 tablespoons sugar

1 tablespoon Accent (optional)

4 cups Converted (parboiled) rice

2 cups finely chopped green bell peppers

2 cups finely chopped onions

5 tablespoons butter

continued...

5. Stir the rice and check to see if it is done or if you need to add more of the tomato sauce to keep it moist while it finishes cooking. It may need to bake for as long as 1 hour and 15 minutes. The smaller baking dishes will take 30 to 45 minutes. Serve warm.

TIPS

• If there's any leftover tomato sauce, pour it into a freezer bag to freeze for a small batch of red rice.

• The red rice freezes well in a sealed plastic container. Thaw it overnight in the refrigerator. Break up any frozen bits with your fingers, put it in a baking dish, and sprinkle a little water over the top to moisten. Cover, and reheat at 325 degrees for 20 to 35 minutes, the longer time if any of it's still frozen.

gone-to-glory potato salad

You'll read in cookbooks that you should use red- or white-skinned waxy potatoes for potato salad, but I don't hold with that. In our part of the South we like a softer potato salad, almost like a mash in some places. So I use russets, baking potatoes, to get that consistency. You can use any potatoes, of course, but see how you like it this way. I can almost guarantee you won't have any leftovers.

I never ate potato salad when I was growing up, because of the mayonnaise. The very idea of it didn't agree with me. Then one day I tasted Miracle Whip and loved it. Now people insist that I make this salad—for picnics, parties, and the holidays. Some people even put a scoop of potato salad right in the middle of a serving of gumbo, especially at Christmas.

When I make a batch, I usually start with about thirty pounds of potatoes, or I won't have enough for all my family and friends. But this smaller batch will taste just as good as mine. **SERVES 8**

1. Have a bowl of cold water ready. Cut the potatoes lengthwise in half, then cut each half in thirds. Slice the cut-up potatoes into ¾-inch chunks and put them in the bowl of cold water as you go, then drain them.

2. In a large pot, cover the potato chunks with cold water and bring to a boil. Add a little salt once the water boils and cook over medium heat until the potatoes are just tender through but not soft. Dump the potatoes into a colander and let them cool in it.

3. When the potatoes are cool, put them in a large bowl and add everything else. Mix the potato salad with your hands—really, this makes a big difference—gently but thoroughly. Taste for seasoning and correct it if necessary.

4. Cover the potato salad and chill for at least 30 minutes. Overnight is fine. Serve cold.

6–8 medium russet potatoes, peeled

Salt

5 large hard-boiled eggs (see Box, page 165), chopped into ½-inch pieces

1 celery rib, finely chopped (optional)

½ cup finely diced green bell pepper

⅓ cup finely chopped onion

1½ cups Miracle Whip or mayonnaise

1½ teaspoons Dijon mustard

2 tablespoons sweet pickle relish

2 teaspoons Dora's Savannah Seasoning (page 79)

1 teaspoon Accent (optional)

Heaping ½ teaspoon paprika

⅛ teaspoon plus 2 dashes Texas Pete or other hot sauce

green pea salad with dill

This very simple, no-cooking, make-it-all-ahead pea salad tastes so green and fresh that it's like a breath of fresh air. It's great with fish or chicken, actually almost anything, and it will sit on a buffet table for a long time without looking sad. People always say, "What *is* this?" And after a while they'll ask, "Could you please bring along that pea salad?"

Read the recipe through before you make it, because you need to get it started a couple of days ahead. **SERVES 6**

1. Put everything in a bowl and mix together gently with your hands. Cover and refrigerate overnight.

2. Taste the salad in the morning for seasoning and to see if it needs more herbs. Add more if you need to and return it to the fridge.

3. About ½ hour before you plan to serve it, remove the dish from the refrigerator and uncover it.

1 (1-pound) bag frozen petite peas, defrosted overnight in the fridge (see Tip)

Scant ½ cup Duke's mayonnaise, mixed with ½ teaspoon sugar (see Tips)

½ cup shredded cheddar cheese

5 green onions (scallions), white and firm green parts, chopped fine

About ¼ cup snipped fresh dill, or more to taste

2 tablespoons chopped fresh mint or tarragon, or more to taste (optional)

Salt and ground black pepper to taste

TIPS

• The only trick is to buy the frozen petite peas ahead and start with the salad 2 days before you plan to serve it—you defrost the peas the first overnight, then let the salad season the second overnight, and serve it on the third day.

• Duke's mayonnaise is good with the sweet peas. Any mayonnaise will be good, though. Check the ingredient list on the container; if it has sugar, omit it here.

• The salad is fine made with just dill, but if you have some mint or tarragon, that's even better. You can scatter more snipped herbs on top of the salad when you serve it. Snipped chives are also very good in the salad, and if they're blooming, you can scatter some of the pinky-purple flowers on top when you serve it.

TIP

If you're in a huge rush, you can thaw the peas at room temperature, but they won't have the same just-picked texture.

mustardy brown-sugar baked beans

I make this dish with canned pork and beans because they give me a big head start on flavor. That way, I can add what I want to bring them up to where I want them, and have delicious baked beans in just an hour and a half.

If you need to bring a covered dish somewhere, this is the easiest one I know to put together, and everyone loves it. I usually bake it in a picnic-size aluminum baking pan covered with foil.

This recipe makes a *lot* of baked beans, but you won't have any trouble finding people to finish them off—they're that good. SERVES 25 TO 30

1. Set the oven to 350 degrees. Have ready a 20-x-12-inch baking dish (see Tip) with a lid (or you can use aluminum foil to make your own cover).

2. Combine everything but the butter in a large bowl and mix well. Spoon the beans into the baking dish. Scatter the butter pieces evenly over the top of the beans and cover with the lid or foil.

3. Slide the dish into the oven and bake for 1½ hours. Serve warm, or let cool, then cover and refrigerate to reheat later.

4. Before you reheat the beans, check to see if they seem dry on top. If they do, sprinkle a little water on top before covering and reheating in a 350-degree oven for 25 minutes.

1 (7-pound) or 7 (15-ounce) can(s) pork and beans

1½ cups diced onions

1½ cups diced green bell peppers

7 thick bacon slices, fried and crumbled, plus the grease

2½ cups packed light brown sugar

¼ cup yellow mustard

¼ cup honey

1 stick (8 tablespoons) butter, chilled and cut into small pieces

TIP

To cut this recipe in half, just halve all the ingredients, use an 8-x-10-inch baking dish, and bake for 45 minutes.

black-eyed peas

These are *the* peas in the South, unless you count the Lowcountry red field peas we like to use for Hoppin' John, the good-luck dish you are *required* to serve on New Year's Day. (The cooking directions for red peas are almost the same—see below.)

Like all peas and beans, black-eyes are even better the next day, as long as they're properly seasoned and you haven't overcooked them, so it's worth making enough for two days. By not overcooked, I mean the peas should be firm but tender, so check them often as they near the end of their cooking time. SERVES 8

1. Pick over the peas and remove any stones or broken peas. Rinse and soak them, completely covered in cold water, until you're ready to cook them. (I don't soak them overnight.)

2. Fry the hog jowl or bacon pieces slowly in a deep heavy pot with a lid. When they're golden brown, scoop them out of the pot with a slotted spoon and set aside; leave the cooking fat in the pot.

3. Add the hot water and everything else, including the drained peas, to the pot and raise the heat. When the water comes to a rapid boil, add the hog jowl or bacon pieces, cover, and cook over medium-low heat for about 1 hour and 45 minutes. Check the pot beginning at 1 hour and 15 minutes to see if the peas are firm-tender—as soon as they are, take them off the heat.

4. Serve the peas hot with their potlikker, save for the next day, or use to make a dish of Hoppin' John (page 179).

1½ cups (½ pound) dried black-eyed peas

6 slices smoked hog jowl or thick-sliced slab bacon, cut into 2-inch pieces

8 cups hot water

Pinch of sugar

1 tablespoon Dora's Savannah Seasoning (page 79)

3 chicken bouillon cubes

1 garlic clove, chopped

TIP

If you happen to cook the peas in a large cast-iron pot, take them, and their potlikker, out of the pot as soon as they're done. If they sit for any length of time in the pot, the pot stays so hot that it will cook the potlikker away. A lot of people love the potlikker over rice almost more than the peas themselves.

TIP

If you have some red field peas, which appear in our grocery stores for a short time from fall to early winter, or the very special Gullah peas called Sea Island red peas (available from Anson Mills; see Sources, page 263), use 2 cups peas and plan on cooking them a bit longer.

hoppin' john

This favorite dish has been taken up all over the South, but it comes from the Low-country. We wouldn't dream of passing New Year's Day without it, because your luck in the coming year depends on it. Also, it's just delicious, so good you'll want to serve it all year long.

You'll notice I use Converted (parboiled) rice here. I say you can't go wrong with it; you always get the perfect texture. SERVES 4 TO 6

1. You can start cooking the peas before you cook the rice, or reheat the peas (see Tip, opposite page) before adding to the rice if you make them ahead.

2. Add the rice, water, and salt to a 2-quart saucepan and bring to a rapid boil over high heat. Cover, reduce the heat to medium-low, and cook for 45 minutes to an hour. At about 35 minutes, uncover the pot and stir in the garlic. Scatter the onion and green pepper over the top of the rice—don't stir them in. Continue to cook, uncovered, until the rice is cooked through.

3. Measure the cooked rice into a bowl or serving dish and add an equal amount of cooked peas. Gently mix the two together. Serve right away, or cool, refrigerate, and reheat the following day.

- 1 recipe Black-Eyed Peas; or use red peas; see opposite
- 1½ cups Converted (parboiled) rice, rinsed under cold running water
- 3 cups water
- ½ teaspoon salt
- 1 garlic clove, chopped fine
- ½ small onion, chopped fine
- ½ green bell pepper, chopped fine

> **TIP**
>
> For proper Hoppin' John, there should be roughly equal parts peas and rice. The amount of rice here will give you the necessary 5 cups cooked rice, but you may have to take away as much as a cup of the peas to get 5 cups cooked peas.

squash casserole

If you're not Southern, you probably haven't had squash casserole, but in the South, this creamy, sweet, crookneck squash dish with its crunchy, cheesy topping is a big thing. I like to use both yellow squash and zucchini for more flavor and color. If your family usually makes a face when you serve squash, that won't happen when you serve this casserole. **SERVES 4 TO 6**

1. Set the oven to 350 degrees.

2. Put the squash slices in a large saucepan and cover with water. Bring to a boil, then reduce to a simmer and cook just until the squash is tender, a few minutes. Drain well and when it cools a little, squeeze the squash dry and set aside.

3. Melt 4 tablespoons of the butter in a large skillet over medium heat. Add the onion and bell peppers and cook until soft, 6 to 7 minutes.

4. Scrape the onion and peppers into a large bowl. Add the yellow squash, zucchini, sour cream, cheese, and seasoning. Put the squash mixture into a 9-x-7-inch or an 8-x-8-inch casserole dish.

5. Melt the remaining 2 tablespoons butter. In a small bowl, combine the cracker crumbs and fried onions with the melted butter and mix well.

6. Spread the cracker mixture over the casserole and bake until golden brown, 25 to 30 minutes. Serve hot or warm.

2 pounds crookneck squash, cut into ½-inch-thick slices

1 pound zucchini, cut into ½-inch-thick slices

¾ stick (6 tablespoons) butter

1 large onion, chopped

1 large green bell pepper, chopped

½ large orange bell pepper, chopped

1 (8-ounce) container sour cream

1½ cups shredded cheddar cheese

Dora's Savannah Seasoning (page 79) to taste

1 cup crushed Ritz crackers

½ cup canned fried onions, crushed

TIP

Squash can hold a lot of water, so you really want to be sure you squeeze it well after you drain it so the casserole won't be watery.

A Real Southern Cook

broccoli casserole

A lot of people won't eat broccoli, but I don't know anyone who doesn't like this casserole. You can definitely taste the broccoli, but it's lifted up by the seasonings, the creamy mushrooms, and the cheeses and crackers.   SERVES 6

1. Set the water to boil with 1 tablespoon of the Savannah seasoning in a large pot over high heat.

2. Meantime, set the oven to 350 degrees and adjust a rack position to the top third. Butter a 2-quart (9-x-9-inch) shallow baking dish and set aside.

3. Once the water is boiling, drop in the broccoli, bring back to a boil, and boil for 5 minutes. Drain the broccoli in a large colander and put it in a large bowl.

4. Add the cream of mushroom soup, cheeses, onion, eggs, and the remaining ½ teaspoon Savannah seasoning and mix well. Scrape the broccoli mixture into the baking dish.

5. Crunch up the crackers inside their sleeve and scatter the crumbs evenly on top of the casserole—you may not need all of them to just cover the top. Drizzle the melted butter on top of the crumbs.

6. Bake the casserole until the top is golden brown, about 15 minutes. Serve hot or reheat later (about 10 minutes in a 325-degree oven).

3 quarts water

1 tablespoon plus ½ teaspoon Dora's Savannah Seasoning (page 79)

8 cups very coarsely chopped broccoli (about 2 large heads; see Tip)

2¼ cups canned condensed cream of mushroom soup

1 cup shredded sharp cheddar cheese

1 scant cup shredded Colby Jack cheese

½ cup chopped onion

2 large eggs, beaten with a fork

1 long sleeve Ritz crackers (about 26)

1 tablespoon butter, melted

TIP

If you haven't been using the stalks of broccoli, you have a treat coming. They have a sweet, delicate flavor, quite different from the broccoli flowers and smaller stems. Peel away the tough outer layer, dice the stalk, and add it to the rest of the broccoli. Or try it on its own, steamed with just salt and pepper, or mashed into a puree with just a little nutmeg.

when company's calling

THE HOLIDAYS ARE A TIME when good cooks get called day and night. People outside the black community don't necessarily know about this, but a lot of cooks make up giant quantities of their specialties and either sell them or trade them, just as the more enterprising slaves did on plantations. I myself have to make about sixty sweet potato pies just to keep my extended family happy, and I might trade one for my friend Edna's pound cake. There are people who specialize in cheesecakes, and others who make famous barbecue or great gumbo. It ends up that a lot of dishes on the holiday table are made outside the home kitchen but are still homemade, which is a great solution to holiday food stress.

A smoked ham with a brown sugar glaze is almost always a centerpiece, but it could also be Sunday Roast Chicken, with a special family heritage side dish like Grandmom Hattie's Dressing. Or, for a really knockout feast, it could be both. Mac 'n' cheese, collard greens, banana pudding, and especially sweet potato pie are all essentials too.

When you're not cooking for a crowd but making an intimate celebration for company, Rosemary Cornish Hens are a perfect choice, but also think about Crab Cakes (page 140). For a party, I'd go with Party Pot Roast, which is easy on the cook and always a great hit. And I know you're thinking, oh, *she* thinks meatloaf's for company. Yes, I do—the one in this chapter feeds a crowd, and I promise you'll get no complaints.

the ham

There are certain times when there just has to be a ham, a really smoky, succulent one, with a brown sugar glaze. One of my pet peeves is that almost no one takes the time to make the ham pretty—and if they do, whoever slices it will usually mess it up by cutting big, thick slices that just don't look nice or taste as good as very thin slices do.

This ham is scored, stuck with some cloves so it has the pattern of a pineapple skin, glazed with brown sugar, and topped off with a touch of pineapple. You could put a whole clove in the middle of each square of fat you've scored on the ham, but although it's pretty, that's a lot of strong clove flavor going into your ham. I put in just a few cloves, still in a pretty pattern, but not too many. And one more thing: There's a bottle of Coke in the bottom of the baking pan to perfume the big piggy as it bakes.

If the ham is properly sliced, you'll be amazed at how many people it will feed. And save the ham bone for making a pot of beans or soup.

SERVES 40, SLICED THIN FOR A BUFFET

1. Set the oven to 350 degrees. Have ready a roasting pan with a roasting rack set inside.

2. There may be some skin on the ham; if there is, cut it away from the fat (see Tips). Score the ham fat to make a diamond pattern and set the ham on the roasting rack.

3. Pour the water into the bottom of the roasting pan and cover the ham and the pan with foil, crimping the foil around the edges of the pan. Bake for 2 hours.

4. After about 1½ hours, remove the pan from the oven, pull back the foil, and spoon out ½ cup ham juice from the bottom of the pan into a saucepan. Work out a pattern and stick the cloves in the middle of some of the scored squares. Replace the foil cover on the pan, and return it to the oven for another ½ hour. Stir the brown sugar and honey into the ham juice in the saucepan. Bring the mixture to a boil over medium heat,

1 whole smoked picnic ham (11–12 pounds)

1 cup water

Small handful of whole cloves

1 cup light brown sugar

3 tablespoons honey

1 (12-ounce) bottle Coca-Cola

1 (8-ounce) can crushed pineapple, drained

stirring, and simmer, uncovered, until thickened, 15 to 20 minutes. Set the glaze aside.

5. After the ham has cooked for 2 hours, remove it from the oven, remove the foil, and remove to a platter; set aside. Drain off all but about 1 cup of the liquid in the pan. Pour the Coke into the pan. Return the ham to the pan and brush the glaze all over it. Spoon the crushed pineapple over the top and sides of the ham. Drizzle any leftover glaze over the ham.

6. Bake the ham, uncovered, for ½ hour. Remove the ham from the oven, cover the pan completely with foil again, and set in a warm place; let the Coke steam its flavor through the ham for 15 minutes.

7. Remove the ham to a serving platter or cutting board. Let rest for at least a half hour, then slice very thin and serve.

TIPS

• The pork skin on the ham is a cook's big treat. Cut away any fat clinging to it, cut into strips, and heat some oil in a deep fryer or a deep skillet. If you're using a skillet, be careful—the skin may start popping, and it's easy to burn yourself. Fry the skin crisp, but don't let it get extra crispy, or it will be hard. Drain on paper towels and eat warm.

• The baked ham will keep, tightly wrapped in the refrigerator, for about 5 days. If you haven't eaten it all or given it away by then, package it up in small servings and store in the freezer.

cheesy meatloaf with mushroom sauce

There's no bread in my meatloaf. And I don't make it in a loaf pan—I never could see the point of that. And it's not made with mixed meats. And it doesn't have tomato sauce in it or on it. So it's not the same old meatloaf. This one looks like a very long, fat loaf of bread, and it's baked naked, no bacon on top, on a baking sheet. It has a deeply satisfying old-school flavor.

It can serve a lot of people but usually everyone wants seconds and then there's no leftovers for sandwiches. You might think the mushroom sauce is just an extra thing to fancy it up, but the sauce is so delicious—it's cheesy too—that you don't want to miss it. The recipe makes a lot of sauce, which is a good thing. If you run out of leftover meatloaf, it's also delicious over broccoli or cauliflower.

SERVES 8 TO 12; MAKES ABOUT 5 CUPS SAUCE

1. To make the meatloaf: Set the oven to 350 degrees. Grease or spray a baking sheet with oil or baking spray.

2. Put the beef and cheese in a very large bowl and add the Lawry's seasoning, salt, granulated garlic, and black pepper. Add the green pepper and onion. Set aside.

3. In a small bowl, whisk the sour cream with the Worcestershire sauce. Crack in the eggs, cutting into the yolks with a wooden spoon to mix them in more easily. Whisk the mixture together well and add it to the meat mixture. Using your hands, mix everything together thoroughly.

4. To be sure the seasoning is right, make a small patty of the meatloaf mixture and cook it in a skillet. Taste it; you may need to add more salt or garlic or something else. Once the seasoning is right, put the meat mixture on the baking sheet and pat it gently into a long oblong loaf about a foot long, 5 inches wide, and 2¼ inches tall. The easiest way to do this is to slap it gently into place.

Meatloaf

- 3 pounds ground beef (20% fat is about right)
- 2 cups thickly shredded mild or sharp cheddar cheese
- 1 teaspoon Lawry's Seasoned Salt
- 1 scant teaspoon salt, or more to taste
- 1 teaspoon granulated garlic, or more to taste
- ½ teaspoon freshly ground black pepper, or to taste
- 1 cup finely chopped green bell pepper
- 1 cup finely chopped yellow onion
- ½ cup sour cream
- 2 tablespoons Worcestershire sauce
- 3 large eggs

continued...

5. Bake the meatloaf for about 1 hour. When it's done, the top will be browned and the meatloaf will feel firm when you pat the top of it. Remove the meatloaf from the oven and let stand, still on the baking sheet, for at least 15 minutes.

6. Meantime, make the mushroom sauce: Heat up the mushroom soup in a large saucepan, uncovered, over medium-low heat. Don't let it heat to the point that it makes a popping sound; turn the heat down if it does. Add the salt, garlic, and pepper and mix well with a wooden spoon. Slowly add the cream, whisking as you go, and cook briefly over low heat; you just want to get it hot. Taste it; you may need to add a little more salt. Slowly add the cheese, whisking until smooth. Keep in a warm oven until ready to serve.

7. Slice the meatloaf and serve with the sauce spooned over each slice.

Mushroom Sauce

- 1 (14½-ounce) can condensed cream of mushroom soup
- ¼ teaspoon salt, or more to taste
- ¼ heaped teaspoon minced garlic
- ¼ teaspoon ground black pepper
- 1¾ cups heavy cream
- 2 cups thinly shredded mild or sharp cheddar cheese

TIP

Slices of leftover meatloaf are wonderful reheated on the grill. Drizzle a little of the hot mushroom sauce over the top of each slice.

party pot roast

This recipe makes a lot of pot roast. I find it works best to start with two roasts and cook them together in the roasting pan. They look gorgeous before they head for the oven, surrounded by wreaths of red, green, and yellow pepper strips; bright orange carrots; and lots of other vegetables. Once the dish is cooked, it's not as stunning, but it's still very appealing in its own way—and the aroma is something special all by itself.

You can get this made early in the day or even the day before, and the flavors will only improve with the extra time. You can also make just one 3½- to 4-pound pot roast. Cut the recipe in half, but keep the roasting time the same.

SERVES ABOUT 16

1. Set the oven to 350 degrees. Have ready a large roasting pan with a lid, or use heavy-duty foil to cover the pan.

2. Mix the Savannah seasoning with the Accent, if using. Season the pot roasts all over with the seasoning mixture. Stir the bouillon cubes into the hot water and set aside.

3. Mix the carrots, celery, and peppers together in a large bowl. Put half of them in the roasting pan and nestle the roasts into the vegetables. Add the rest of the vegetable mixture around the roasts. Scatter the potatoes and onion around the meat. Tuck the bay leaves in with the vegetables all around the pan. Pour the beef bouillon evenly around the roasts.

4. Cover the roasting pan tightly with the lid or foil. Roast until the meat is completely tender, 2 to 2½ hours. Remove the roasts and vegetables to one or two platters and pick out and discard the bay leaves. Keep the roasts and vegetables warm under foil while you make the gravy.

5. To make the gravy: Pour the pan juices into a large saucepan and bring to a boil over medium-high heat. Shake the flour and the water together well in a sealed glass jar until there are no lumps. Pour the slurry into the boiling juices and

2 tablespoons Dora's Savannah Seasoning (page 79)

1 tablespoon Accent (optional)

1 (7-pound) chuck roast, cut into 2 equal pieces, or 2 (3½-pound) roasts

3 beef bouillon cubes

5 cups hot water

8–10 carrots, peeled

4 celery ribs, cut on an angle into 1-inch chunks

3 medium bell peppers— red, green, yellow, and/or orange—cut into strips

6 large russet potatoes, peeled, cut lengthwise in half and then crosswise into sixths

1 large onion, cut into wedges

5 bay leaves

Gravy

6 tablespoons all-purpose flour

2 cups water

Salt and ground black pepper to taste

stir constantly until the gravy is thickened and the flour has cooked and browned, 12 to 15 minutes. Taste for seasoning and adjust if necessary.

6. Thinly slice the pot roasts or cut into chunks. Serve the meat and vegetables with the gravy on the side.

> **TIP**
>
> If you make the pot roast a day ahead, you can refrigerate it right in the roasting pan, well covered. Reheat the roast the next day, still covered, at 325 degrees for ½ hour, or until heated through. Remove the meat and vegetables to a serving platter and keep warm while you make the gravy, as above.

sunday roast chicken with herb butter

A fine roasted chicken is the famous Sunday dinner offered to the preacher after church, a sign of welcome and hospitality. I tuck butter mixed with herbs and spice in under the skin so as the chicken roasts, the butter melts to carry the flavors into the meat. A sprinkle of paprika on top of the chicken gives it a rosy glow, and the vegetables roasting all around it give up their juices to a pan sauce. SERVES 6

1. Set the oven to 350 degrees.

2. Rinse the chicken inside and out and pat it dry.

3. In a small bowl, mix the softened butter, thyme, sage, and nutmeg together with a fork. Work the tips of your fingers under the skin of the chicken over the breast, being careful not to puncture the skin. (If you haven't done this before, it can seem kind of difficult, but be brave. Wiggle your fingers around to break any little connecting pieces.) Smear the seasoned butter under the skin over the chicken breast, working your way down to the thighs. Sprinkle the chicken inside and outside with 2 tablespoons of the Savannah seasoning, rubbing it in well.

4. Line the bottom of a large deep casserole dish or a roasting pan with half the onion, celery, and peppers, setting the other half of the vegetables aside. Arrange the chicken, breast side up, on top of the vegetables. Sprinkle the paprika over the chicken and rub it in lightly.

5. Scatter the potatoes and carrots and the rest of the celery, peppers, and onion around the chicken. Sprinkle the remaining ½ teaspoon Savannah seasoning evenly over the vegetables and drizzle the water evenly around the chicken.

6. Roast the chicken for 45 minutes. Give the vegetables a stir, rearranging them so they cook evenly. Roast until a drumstick

1 (5-pound) roasting chicken

2 generous tablespoons butter, softened

¾ teaspoon dried thyme

½ teaspoon dried sage

⅛ teaspoon grated nutmeg

2 tablespoons plus ½ teaspoon Dora's Savannah Seasoning (page 79)

1 medium onion, cut in half and then into half-moons

2 celery ribs, cut on an angle into 1-inch-thick chunks

½ green bell pepper, cut into thin strips

½ yellow bell pepper, cut into thin strips

1 teaspoon paprika

5 medium russet potatoes, peeled and cut into quarters

1 pound baby carrots

½ cup water

wiggles in its knee joint and the juices from the thickest part of the thigh run clear, about another 45 minutes.

7. When the chicken is done, let it rest on a carving board for 20 minutes while you keep the vegetables warm in the pan, stirring them so they pick up the juices left in the pan.

8. Carve the chicken and serve with the vegetables and any pan juices.

TIP

If you happen to have fresh herbs on hand, mince them and use three times the quantity of the dried ones for the herb butter.

rosemary cornish hens for two

Although I'm usually cooking for a lot of people, sometimes it's just one special person, and I want the dinner to be special too. That's when I make these Cornish hens, which are seasoned with lots of rosemary and stuffed with a rice dressing. I use brown rice, but you can use white if you prefer.

The little hens look very cozy in their casserole dish—sometimes I think they look like they're flirting. **SERVES 2**

1. To make the rice: Rinse the rice well in a strainer under hot tap water to get rid of extra starch, then put it in a 2-quart saucepan. Add the chicken stock and salt and bring to a rapid boil over high heat. Cover and cook over medium-low heat for 45 minutes to an hour. Stir the onion, celery, and parsley into the rice and set aside, uncovered, to cool completely.

2. To cook the hens: Set the oven to 350 degrees. Spray a 9-x-13-inch casserole dish with olive oil.

3. Spray the Cornish hens both inside and out with olive oil. Sprinkle them inside and out with the Savannah seasoning and arrange them in the casserole dish. Stuff the hens with some of the rice and spoon 1 teaspoon of the rosemary over each hen, patting it onto the tops and sides. Spoon the remaining rice around the hens. Evenly sprinkle ¼ teaspoon of the paprika onto each hen. Sprinkle the remaining 1 teaspoon rosemary over the rice.

4. Drizzle the chicken stock evenly over the rice in the dish and cover the dish with a lid or foil.

5. Bake the Cornish hens for 1½ hours, or until the juices in the thickest part of the thigh run clear. Serve hot, with the rice on the side.

Rice

- 1 cup brown rice or Converted (parboiled) white rice
- 2½ cups chicken stock (2 cups if using white rice)
- ¼ teaspoon salt
- 1 small onion, diced
- 1 cup diced celery
- 1 tablespoon dried parsley

Hens

- 2 Cornish hens (defrosted if frozen)

  Olive oil in a spray bottle
- 1 tablespoon Dora's Savannah Seasoning (page 79)
- 3 teaspoons dried rosemary, finely crumbled
- ½ teaspoon sweet Spanish smoked paprika, or more to taste
- ⅓ cup chicken stock

grandmom hattie's dressing

If we're having roast turkey, this is one of the side dishes—along with mashed potatoes—that must be on the table. I remember my grandmother making it, and when my daughter sees me making it, it's the real sign the holidays have arrived.

I've never heard of another dressing that has hard-boiled eggs in it. They contribute a creamy, mellow richness and pull all the other flavors together. Another unusual touch is the crisp crunch of the vegetables that go in toward the end of the cooking. This is a cornbread-based dressing, but it's not only cornbread—there's also Pepperidge Farm Herb Seasoned Stuffing. I just can't improve on that, though what makes it really sing is the tasty turkey stock I make from scratch.

There's a trick to the stock, which is using fresh turkey necks. They're usually available in markets during the holidays, or you can special-order them. My daughter loves them so much that she'll steal one right out of the pot. And she's right; if you've never tasted fresh turkey neck, you're in for a major treat when you bite into the dark, succulent meat. I always add at least four of them, so she's happy before dinner and I'm happy at the table. There's not a lot of meat on a turkey neck, but those chopped bits are the special ingredient in the dressing.

Great as it is, this dressing is a *big* production to make, so my sisters and I share the job and make enough for both Christmas and New Year's—that way, the New Year's batch is all done ahead, just waiting in the freezer.

If roast turkey's not on the menu, the dressing is also great with roast chicken.

SERVES 10 TO 12

1. To make the stock: Pour the water into a large pot and add the gizzards and turkey necks. Stir in the Savannah seasoning and bring the pot to a boil over medium-high heat. Turn the heat down to medium and simmer, covered, until the meat is tender, 1 hour and 45 minutes to 2 hours, stirring from time to time. To check, stick a fork into the gizzards; it should go right through if they're tender. Slit the turkey necks to see if the meat tears when you pull it.

2. Add the vegetables to the pot and simmer for 15 minutes more. Remove the turkey necks and let them cool a bit. Strain the stock and let the vegetables and gizzards cool down too.

Stock

3¼ quarts (14 cups) water

1 generous pound chicken gizzards

4 large fresh turkey necks

3 tablespoons Dora's Savannah Seasoning (page 79), or more as needed

1½ cups chopped green bell peppers

1½ cups chopped celery

1½ cups chopped onions

3. Pull the meat off the necks in strips, then chop and set aside. Separate out the gizzards and chop them. You should have about 12 cups stock. If you don't, add water and a little more seasoning until you have 12 cups.

4. To make the dressing: Set the oven at 350 degrees. Grease a 9-x-13-inch baking dish.

5. In a very large bowl, mix together the stuffing, seasonings, hard-boiled eggs, butter, and about 6 cups of the stock. Stir in the vegetables, neck meat, and gizzards. Add about half the cornbread crumbs and more stock as needed; the dressing should be a bit moister than freshly baked cornbread. Taste: Does it need more poultry seasoning, more pepper, more Savannah seasoning, a little more butter? You can keep adding cornbread crumbs as long as you're sure you have enough stock for them. Taste one last time (see Tips). Mix in the beaten eggs. (At this point, you can freeze the dressing in zipper-lock freezer bags or freezer containers for up to 6 months. When you thaw it before baking, if you notice a little water in the container, just add an extra beaten egg to restore the creaminess.)

6. Pile the dressing into the baking dish. Bake until golden brown on top, 30 to 45 minutes. Serve right away, or let it cool and then freeze (see Tips).

Dressing

- 4 cups Pepperidge Farm Herb Seasoned Stuffing

- 2 teaspoons poultry seasoning, or more to taste

- 2 teaspoons Dora's Savannah Seasoning (page 79), or more to taste

- 1 teaspoon dried sage

- 1 teaspoon freshly ground black pepper, or more to taste

- 4 large hard-boiled eggs (see page 165), chopped

- 5½ tablespoons butter, melted, or more as needed

- 1 recipe baked Buttermilk Cornbread (page 64), cooled and crumbled

- 3 large eggs, beaten with a fork

TIPS

• If the dressing tastes perfect before the eggs go in, add a little more of all the seasonings, because the eggs will dilute the flavor a bit.

• Reheat frozen dressing in a covered casserole dish at 325 degrees for 25 minutes, or until heated through.

all sides, all the time

A LOT OF PEOPLE THINK the best thing about Thanksgiving isn't the whopping roast turkey but all the side dishes that come with it, so that your plate is brimming with all kinds of tastes and you go from one to the next, and back again. Now that's a lot like a good Southern country dinner—it's how we eat whenever we can. We love our vegetables, and not just because our mama told us they were good for us (though she did). We love them because they taste so good.

Yes, we fry our vegetables sometimes, and we add a pinch of sugar sometimes, but mostly it's a question of seasoning and understanding how to bring out their personalities. What comes out of the summer garden—the corn, the tomatoes, the okra, the peas and carrots—are among the big treats of the year, but we also love the collards after the first frost, which makes them more tender, and the winter cabbage. If you know how to cook these and season them, they're all delicious. Often that means making a flavorful stock and letting it simmer to bring out the flavor, then cooking the vegetables in it.

Our red clay soil has lots of minerals and other good things that give whatever grows in it deep flavor. You can really see this with sweet potatoes, which can taste all over the map depending on their variety and what soil they were grown in.

My grandparents were poor sharecroppers, but they often ate like kings because they grew everything they ate on their farm up in the country, harvesting it right before they ate it, and because my grandmother was such a great cook.

One summer she managed to put up a thousand glass jars of their produce, so many that my grandfather had to build new shelves around the walls of their big kitchen to hold them all. Aunt Laura remembers these fruits of their labors being so beautiful to look at in their gleaming jars that they almost didn't want to eat them that winter.

After the family moved to Savannah, my father would go to City Market, the famous farmers' market that used to be right in the middle of the city, to choose the best, freshest greens and beans and tomatoes. He'd come home with armloads of collard greens and sackfuls of whatever else looked the best. Aunt Laura says they were shocked at the difference in quality between the city food and the country food, and only the farmers' market had what they were used to back home. When the market was in full harvest, they'd cook it all as fast as they could and freeze it or put it up for the winter.

Daddy and my grandmother both taught me how to recognize the best, and if something doesn't look good at the grocery store, no matter how much I want to cook it, I'll pass it by. And if something looks great that I wasn't planning to cook, I'll grab it. That's when your cooking gets really inspired, when you get lucky with some gorgeous vegetable that's still living and breathing right in front of you, calling your name. Say yes!

country cabbage with smoked bacon

Southerners love cabbage, especially if there's some bacon in it. This version is cooked in my favorite piece of kitchen equipment, a cast-iron skillet. Although the ingredients are simple and humble, the skillet does something magical to them, sweetening the cabbage right up. **SERVES 4**

1. Fry the bacon in a large cast-iron skillet until crisp. Remove the slices to paper towels to drain. Don't pour off the bacon grease.

2. Add the cabbage to the skillet, stir well, and cook the cabbage down, uncovered, stirring occasionally, until it's completely soft and cooked through, about 10 minutes.

3. Stir in the salt and cook for another 5 minutes. Crumble in the bacon. Stir in the butter and taste. You may need to add more salt, but do it little by little and keep tasting until you've got it just right. Serve hot.

4 bacon slices

½ small head cabbage (see Tips), cored, sliced thin, rinsed, and drained well

1 teaspoon salt, or to taste

2 tablespoons butter

TIPS

• You can use either green or red cabbage for this dish. Red has even more vitamins and goodness than green does.

• You can store a whole cabbage for a couple of months in the refrigerator, and assuming you always have bacon on hand, you can make this dish on the spur of the moment. Once you cut the cabbage, though, the other half will keep only a couple of weeks.

coleslaw

There's almost nothing that doesn't go with coleslaw, especially in the summer. This slaw is just a tiny bit sweet, but you can sweeten it up with fruit if you like. If you don't add the fruit, you should use 1½ teaspoons sugar. Also, Duke's mayonnaise contains no sugar, but Blue Plate, Hellmann's, and Miracle Whip all have sugar in them, which may be enough without adding any extra sugar—you'll have to taste.

I like to save a little time by using the fine-cut angel hair cabbage from the market. But you can cut up the cabbage yourself if you want (see Tip). SERVES 4 TO 6

1. In a large bowl, mix the cabbage, carrot, and parsley.

2. In a small bowl, combine the mayonnaise, onion, relish, ½ teaspoon sugar, if you like, the salt, and mustard and mix well.

3. Mix the dressing into the cabbage, stirring well to combine. Cover and refrigerate the coleslaw for at least 4 hours, or overnight, to season.

4. If you're adding the raisins or grapes, stir them in when you're ready to serve. Stir well, taste, and correct the seasonings before serving slightly chilled.

1   (1-pound) package shredded cabbage, preferably angel hair cut (see Tip)

2   tablespoons finely shredded carrot

½   tablespoon chopped fresh parsley

⅓   cup mayonnaise, preferably Duke's

1   tablespoon finely chopped onion

1   tablespoon sweet pickle relish

½–1½ teaspoons sugar, or to taste

¼   teaspoon salt, or more to taste

½   teaspoon yellow mustard

½   cup raisins, or ¾ cup chopped red seedless grapes (optional)

TIP

To shred cabbage yourself for the coleslaw, you'll need ½ medium head. Cut the half in half again, so you have 2 wedges. Next, cut the core out of each wedge and then shred the cabbage by slicing it crosswise as thin as you can manage. The shreds won't be as delicate as the angel hair packages that I like, but as long as you follow the recipe and let the salad sit for at least 4 hours or overnight in the refrigerator, it'll be fine.

all-seasons corn pudding

This rich but light pudding is so quick to make in the blender and so good, even made with frozen corn, that it is my go-to recipe all year long. When you cut into it, there's a wonderful corny fragrance that's released.

There are a few tricks to this dish. Blend the corn mixture as little as possible, so it still has some texture. Use a shallow casserole dish, not deeper than 1½ inches, or it may curdle. And be sure to use a water bath, which is a snap even if you've never done it before. SERVES 6

1. Set the oven to 350 degrees. Butter a shallow (1½-inches-deep) 1½-quart casserole dish and set aside. Have ready a slightly larger shallow dish or baking pan for the water bath.

2. Put 2 cups of the corn, the cream, milk, eggs, sugar, and salt into a blender and blend for just a few seconds, no more than 5 seconds. Pour the mixture into the casserole dish and scatter the remaining corn kernels evenly over the top. Add a few grinds of black pepper and sprinkle several pinches of grated nutmeg evenly over the top of the pudding.

3. Put the casserole dish inside the larger dish. Carefully pour warm water into the larger dish until it comes about 1 inch up the sides of the smaller casserole. Bake until a table knife inserted into the center of the pudding comes out clean, about 1 hour. Serve hot.

2½ cups fresh or defrosted frozen corn kernels (see Tip)

1 cup heavy cream

¼ cup milk

3 large eggs

1 tablespoon sugar

1 teaspoon salt

Freshly ground black pepper to taste

Grated nutmeg to taste

TIP

If you're using frozen corn, look for white shoepeg corn kernels, which are tasty.

TIP

To use corn on the cob, 5 or 6 ears will give you about 2½ cups. To get the kernels off, stand each cob pointy end up in a wide, shallow dish. Holding it by the point, scrape down to the fat end of the cob with a serrated knife, letting the kernels fall into the dish. Scrape down again with the back of the knife to get more of the milky liquid.

lima bean stew with okra

The combination of baby limas and okra is one of my favorites. This stew is flavored with a stock you make from smoked turkey wings and fatback. It's best when fresh okra is in season, but it's also good with frozen okra in the winter.

Check out Talking About Okra (page 208), which will tell you everything you need to know. **SERVES 8 TO 10**

1. In an 8-quart stockpot, bring the water, turkey wings, fatback, seasoned salt, and pepper to a boil over medium-high heat. Turn the heat down to a simmer and let the stock bubble away, uncovered, for 1½ hours. After 45 minutes, add the fatback.

2. Add the lima beans and butter and cook for 15 minutes. Add the okra and cook until tender, about 15 minutes more. Check for seasoning.

3. Ladle the stew into warm bowls of rice.

4½ quarts water

½ pound smoked turkey wings, ham hocks, or kielbasa

1 tablespoon Lawry's Seasoned Salt, or more to taste

½ teaspoon ground black pepper, or more to taste

3 (1½-inch-thick) pieces fatback (see Tips)

2 (1-pound) bags frozen baby lima beans

1 stick (8 tablespoons) butter

1 pound fresh okra pods, trimmed, or frozen okra, defrosted

Foolproof Rice (page 220), for serving

TIPS

• In Savannah, fatback cut in blocks has disappeared from the market, and instead, we get strips of fatback with too much skin. If you can get the block version, cut it into pieces and add it to the stew.

• To serve the stew as a side dish, use a slotted spoon to lift the vegetables and pork out of the stock.

talking about okra

If you think you hate okra, maybe what you had wasn't the best okra. Or maybe you've never had it cooked right, so it's not slimy or stringy. Here's what you need to know:

• Choose the best. Pick up an okra pod and check to see that the skinny tip on the end is flexible—this is the best sign of tenderness. You can also stick your thumbnail or fingernail into the side of a pod—it should slide right in. (The only trouble is that you ruin the pod once you stick it with your nail, so use this trick only as a backup.) If you have to use any pressure at all to move the tip or to puncture the pod, avoid that batch. Daddy taught me these tricks, and he said it's essential to use them because okra in stores is machine-picked whether it's ready or not. Those sturdy okra pods will still be hard once they're cooked, and then they'll turn stringy. Just one hard pod can ruin your whole dish.

• Even if it's tender, don't buy any okra that's not pretty. Bright green is what you want, and there shouldn't be any brown on the pods.

• Giant okra pods aren't the best ones. If they're longer than your longest finger, pass them by.

• If all the okra is hard or ugly, move on to frozen, which is reliable.

• Once you have the right okra, treat it right. There's always a little stem left on the raw pods and you should trim it, but just a little bit. Don't cut down below the stem into the little skirt that tops the pod, or it will open up too much in the cooking and turn slimy.

Now your okra will be perfect.

skillet okra with onion

I love okra cooked with bacon and onion, and using frozen pods means you can make this dish all year long. You can serve it over rice or not, as you like.

SERVES 6

1. Fry the bacon in a large skillet. When it's crisp, remove it to paper towels to drain. Don't pour off the bacon grease.

2. Add the okra rings to the bacon grease in the skillet and season with a little salt and pepper. Cook, uncovered, over medium-low heat for 20 minutes, stirring almost constantly for the first 6 to 7 minutes, then frequently. Add the onion and butter and crumble the bacon on top of the okra. Stir well, cover, and simmer over medium-low heat for ½ hour, giving the okra a stir every 10 minutes or so.

3. Serve hot, over rice if you like.

5 bacon slices

6 cups (one 28-ounce package) frozen okra rings (don't defrost)

Salt and ground black pepper

½ cup chopped onion

3 tablespoons butter

Foolproof Rice (page 220), for serving (optional)

simple smoky okra

If you're grilling, it would be a shame not to grill your okra too. Everyone adores this smoky okra, especially kids. Choose tender pods, and they will never be stringy. If your grill is small, grill the okra before you grill the main course and put it in a deep serving bowl—the okra doesn't need to be hot. SERVES 4 TO 6

1. Trim the okra stems (see page 208) and rinse the pods. Dry the okra on kitchen towels and arrange in a single layer on a baking sheet. Brush well with olive oil all over.

2. You can skewer the okra if you like, but they'll be smokier if you just lay them on the grill or, if they're small enough to fall through the grill grates, put them in a grilling pan. Give them about 4 minutes per side, turning once, or until they are tender.

3. Remove from the grill and salt generously. Serve warm or at room temperature.

1 pound tender okra

Olive oil, for brushing the okra

Salt, preferably a flaky salt like Maldon, to taste

TIPS

• Make this only when you find tender, pretty okra pods at the market. Though frozen is usually fine, it won't work with this.

• You can also roast the okra. Set the oven to 425 degrees and line a baking sheet with foil or parchment paper. Trim and wash the okra (see page 208), put it in a bowl, and drizzle with olive oil. Turn the okra in the bowl with your hands to cover all the pods with the oil. Scatter the okra in a single layer on the pan and roast, turning once, until its ribs are browned. Start checking at 4 minutes per side, then sprinkle with the smoky salt while still hot.

• I've tried flavoring the olive oil with garlic and smoky paprika, but the seasoning seems to get lost in the smoke. Then I came up with the idea of making a little seasoning mix to sprinkle on the okra *after* grilling, and it's the ticket. Put about ½ teaspoon smoky paprika (see Sources, page 263), 2 tablespoons toasted benne (sesame) seeds, and ¾ teaspoon really good salt, something flaky like Maldon salt, in a small bowl or a mortar, if you have one. Then, with the handle of a wooden spoon or the pestle, crush everything together a bit. When the okra comes off the grill, sprinkle it freely with the salt mix. You can also make up a double batch and use it later on roasted green beans or other vegetable dishes to add a little zip to them. Just use it up in a week or two so the benne seeds don't spoil.

bringing on the smoke

So many Southern recipes begin with the direction to fry some bacon in a skillet. What you're really after is the flavor left in the bacon grease, that great back taste of sweet smokiness and porky goodness. Of course we love the bacon too, and I always tell people that it's fine to eat a slice or two of the cooked bacon while you're working on the rest of the recipe—who can resist?

There are a lot of other good sources of smokiness, though—and they do *not* include liquid smoke in a bottle. Often when I'm making slow-cooked vegetables or starches, I'll add something like a smoked turkey wing or pig's tail to the pot. For quicker-cooking vegetables and sides, I start by making a stock, simmering the smoked meaty parts with seasonings for about an hour, then add the vegetables to cook at the very end. It's not as instant as a little bacon grease in the skillet, but it's pretty easy and it makes all the difference.

The meaty bits that I use in my recipes may not all be in your local grocery store, so here are some other possibilities. These are all more or less interchangeable, but smoked turkey parts or sausage will give you a lighter stock, while things like pigs' tails and ham hocks will make a stronger stock.

- Smoked turkey wing (just one will do)
- Smoked turkey neck
- A handful of smoked turkey sausage slices (such as Hillshire Farms)
- About 3 sliced smoked pigs' tails
- Smoked ham hock
- A few chunks of smoked pork belly (unsliced bacon)
- A handful of smoked kielbasa slices

Once the stock is made, you can pull off any extra grease with ice cubes before you add the vegetables: Put some ice cubes in the stock, and the grease will harden around them. As soon as it does, scoop out the ice cubes and hardened fat.

A little smoked Spanish paprika, sweet or hot (see Sources, page 263), adds a subtle smoky flavor to almost anything savory.

bright peppers salad

I love the happy colors of bright bell peppers, so I decided to create a whole salad with all different colors, sparked up with some red onions and fresh green herbs. It's gorgeous to look at, great for any season, and seems to go with anything else you're serving. It can travel perfectly and sit on a buffet table for hours.

You can use just red, yellow, and orange peppers, or add a green and even a purple one if they're in the market. They all have very slightly different tastes, so more colors are not only more beautiful, they also make the flavors of the salad a little more interesting.   **SERVES 6**

1. Combine the pepper strips and onion in a large bowl and toss with the vinegar. Set aside for 10 minutes or up to ½ hour.

2. Add the olive oil and salt and pepper to taste. Toss well and taste for seasoning. Scatter the herbs over the peppers and onions and toss together. Taste again for seasoning and serve.

5 bell peppers of many colors, cut into thin slices (see Tips)

½ medium red onion, cut into thin half-moons

2 tablespoons champagne vinegar, rice vinegar, or other mild white vinegar

5 tablespoons olive oil

Salt and ground black pepper to taste

A large handful of chopped mixed fresh herbs of your choice: parsley, dill, chives, and/or mint

TIPS

• The easiest way to cut up bell peppers is to stand each one up and cut down the four side walls next to the stem so you get 4 large pieces. Remove any seeds and inner membranes.

• If you have leftovers, they're great chopped into chicken salad the next day.

cheater's pickles

These fresh, almost-instant pickles start off with the cucumber slices getting a big chill with a little bit of sugar, which draws out some of their water. Then just a splash of vinegar and a little salt, and you've got a really refreshing side dish for barbecues, picnics, or anything fried. They're great plain, but you can add snipped dill, chives, or mint, or even some thin-sliced Vidalia onion. SERVES 6 TO 8

1. Cut off the ends of the cucumbers and use the tines of a fork to draw long stripes down their lengths. Slice the cucumbers like bread-and-butter pickles, about ⅛ inch thick, and pile them into a large shallow bowl. Sprinkle the sugar over the cucumbers and stir it in well. Scatter the ice cubes over the cucumbers and cover the bowl loosely with plastic wrap. Chill in the freezer for ½ hour.

2. Drain the cucumbers in a colander and pat dry with a clean kitchen towel. Put the cucumbers in a bowl, sprinkle the vinegar evenly over them, and stir well. Add the salt and pepper, if using, and stir well to combine. Toss in the herbs, if using, and the onions, if using. Refrigerate until ready to serve. They'll still be good the next day, though not quite as crisp.

2 English cucumbers (the long ones; see Tip)

2 tablespoons sugar

Handful of ice cubes

¼ cup rice vinegar, champagne vinegar, apple cider vinegar, or distilled white vinegar

Several pinches of flaky salt, such as Maldon

Several grinds of black pepper (optional)

2 tablespoons snipped fresh dill, mint, or chives, or a mixture (optional)

½ Vidalia onion, sliced into thin half-moons (optional)

> **TIP**
>
> English cucumbers don't have a lot of seeds, but garden cucumbers and Kirbys (bumpy-looking pickling cucumbers) actually taste better, though they're not always available. If the cucumbers are seedy, cut them lengthwise in half and scoop out the seeds with a spoon. Slice into half-moons and proceed with the recipe. About 10 Kirbys equal 2 English cucumbers.

creamed potatoes

These spuds are mashed potatoes, but also a little different. They're cooked in bouillon, which gives them a more interesting flavor. You can mash them roughly or well, as you like. **SERVES 4 TO 6**

1. If the potatoes are medium or large, cut them lengthwise in half and then in thirds, so you have 6 chunks each. If they're small, cut each in half and then in half again, so you have 4 chunks each.

2. Bring the water to a boil in a large pot and when it boils, add the bouillon cubes and salt, stirring well. Drop in the potato chunks and gently boil, uncovered, until tender, 20 to 25 minutes.

3. Drain the potatoes in a colander in the sink and dump them into a large bowl. Add the half-and-half and butter and mash with a potato masher, scooping them up often with a mixing spoon. You can mash them very well or a bit coarsely, however you like them. Season to taste with more salt, if needed, and pepper and serve immediately.

2 pounds russet potatoes, peeled (see Tips)

6 cups water

4 chicken bouillon cubes

1 teaspoon salt, or more to taste

⅓ cup half-and-half, warmed

1 tablespoon butter, softened

Ground black pepper to taste

TIPS

• You can use any size potato, but I usually just count 1 medium potato per person, plus 1 extra—what I call a lucky potato for the pot. If they're large, you can skip the extra potato.

• This recipe is a bit rich, so a little goes a long way.

sweet potato casserole

There are hundreds of versions of sweet potato casseroles, but this one is a bit unusual because it includes coconut milk. You don't really taste it—it just adds an interesting creamy flavor—but if you'd rather not use it, you can use a stick of softened butter instead. Do be sure to include the crumble topping, however—people just love that.

You can roast the sweet potatoes several days ahead and keep them in the refrigerator, well covered, until you're ready to make the casserole (see Tips).

SERVES 6 TO 8

1. Set the oven to 350 degrees. Butter a 1½-quart baking dish.

2. Cut the sweet potatoes lengthwise in half and gently scoop out the flesh. Mash them in a large bowl. Add the sugar, cinnamon, nutmeg, coconut milk or butter, and orange extract or zest and mix well. Once the mixture is smooth, dump the sweet potatoes into the buttered baking dish and spread evenly.

3. To make the crumble: Put all the ingredients in a medium bowl and blend them with your fingers. It's ready when you've worked it enough so that a fistful of the crumble dropped from about 8 inches above the bowl falls in a big lump without cracking. Distribute the crumble evenly over the top of the casserole, about half an inch thick.

4. Slide the dish into the oven and bake until the sweet potatoes are heated through and the crumble has crisped a bit, about 25 minutes. Serve hot.

5 large sweet potatoes (see Tips), roasted and chilled

¼ cup white sugar

1 tablespoon ground cinnamon

2 teaspoons grated nutmeg

1 (13.5-ounce) can coconut milk, stirred well, or 1 stick (8 tablespoons) butter, softened

½ teaspoon pure orange extract, or 1 teaspoon grated orange zest

The Crumble

1 cup light brown sugar

¼ cup all-purpose flour

2 tablespoons butter, softened

½ cup chopped walnuts or pecans

TIPS

• If you have a choice, get Beauregard, Covington, Jewel, or Garnet sweet potatoes.

• Roast the sweet potatoes at 350 degrees until very tender, about 1 hour. Then let them cool. I peel mine hot, but refrigerating makes them even easier to peel.

TIP

If you have Scrumptious Bacon (page 55) on hand, crumble some of that into the topping for an even bigger treat.

foolproof rice

Our family has always loved rice with everything, because for generations we've lived in the Lowcountry, the coastal area of South Carolina and Georgia where rice was first grown in America. The Lowcountry is also the home of the famous Carolina Gold rice, a luxury rice with a delicate taste.

Over the years I've discovered that the best, most foolproof rice is Converted, a long-grain rice that is also called parboiled. It's a hard rice, so it cooks a little longer, no matter what the package directions say. You just can't go wrong with it. Follow my instructions, and you'll have perfectly cooked, fluffy rice with separate grains and no gumminess. Not everyone rinses the rice very well to get all the extra starch off it, but I do, and I swear it makes a difference. **SERVES 6**

1. You can rinse the rice in a 2-quart saucepan with a lid or in a strainer under the tap. If you're rinsing in the saucepan, put the rice in, then add hot but not scalding water to come almost to the top of the pan and swish it around with your hand for a minute, rubbing the rice grains together gently. Carefully pour off the water when it's white, using your fingers to hold back the rice. Repeat three times—you won't get the water to run clear, but it will be much less cloudy after the third time. Or, if you're using a strainer, lift the rice up gently with your hand so the hot tap water can get all through it and rub the grains together gently. Rinse for a minute or two, until the water is much less cloudy. Add the rice to the saucepan.

2. Pour in the 4 cups water and stir in the salt. Boil, uncovered, over medium-high heat for 20 to 30 minutes, until the water is almost gone.

3. Cut the butter into 8 equal pieces and drop it evenly over the top of the rice—a half stick is the minimum, I usually use a bit more. Cover the rice and let it simmer over low heat until the water is gone, 15 to 20 minutes. Check with a fork to be sure the rice is tender.

4. Serve hot.

1½ cups Converted (parboiled) rice

4 cups water

1 teaspoon salt, or to taste

½ stick (4 tablespoons) butter, or more if you like

sweet stewed tomatoes

Stewed tomatoes may sound kind of everyday ho-hum, but this dish is a good example of what I mean when I say real Southern cooking is bursting with flavor. It's a very simple dish, served over rice in a bowl, but oh my, it could bring you to your knees. And because it's made with ingredients you almost always have on hand, it's a great emergency light meal or a fine side dish.

It may seem like there's too much sugar here, and you can use less if you like, but try it my way first. SERVES 6

1. In a 2-quart saucepan, heat the tomatoes with their juice over medium heat until bubbling. Add the chicken bouillon, sugar, salt, seasoned salt, and pepper, cover, and simmer for 15 minutes.

2. Meantime, cook the bacon in a large skillet over medium heat until crispy. Drain on paper towels. Measure out 2 tablespoons of the bacon grease and set it aside (save the rest in the refrigerator for something else). Save the cooked bacon for another meal or chop it for adding to the tomatoes just before serving.

3. After the tomatoes have cooked for 15 minutes, add the onion and the reserved 1 tablespoon bacon grease, cover, and simmer for another 20 minutes.

4. Add the butter. If you are adding the chopped bacon, now's the time. Give the tomatoes a good stir and taste for seasoning.

5. Serve the tomatoes hot over hot rice in a bowl.

1 (28-ounce) can diced tomatoes, with their juice

1 chicken bouillon cube, dissolved in ½ cup hot water

Scant ⅓ cup sugar

½ teaspoon salt

½ teaspoon Lawry's Seasoned Salt

¼ teaspoon ground black pepper

6 bacon slices

1 medium onion, coarsely chopped

2 tablespoons butter

Foolproof Rice (opposite), for serving

TIP

You can make this using about 2 pounds fresh plum-type tomatoes. To peel them first, bring a large pot of water to a boil. Cut out the cores from the stem ends and cut a little X into the pointy ends. Drop the tomatoes into the boiling water for about 30 seconds, then scoop them out and drop them into a bowl of icy-cold water. The skins will slip right off.

TIP

Leftover tomatoes are delicious the next day. Once they've cooled, store them in a covered container in the refrigerator before reheating.

crookneck squash with bacon

My beloved grandmother used to make this stew when yellow crookneck squash was in the market, and it was almost the only dish I didn't like. I'd just pick out the bacon and try to avoid the squash.

It wasn't until I started working with Paula Deen that I finally came to love squash. Resurrecting my grandmother's recipe was a real challenge, because I'd never watched while she cooked it. But finally I got it, and this is exactly how she did it. **SERVES 4 TO 6**

1. Fry the bacon in a large skillet. When it's cooked, remove to paper towels to drain. Don't pour off the bacon grease.

2. Add the squash and salt and pepper to the bacon grease in the skillet, stir well, and cook over medium-low heat, stirring frequently, until the squash is very tender, about 20 minutes; don't let it brown.

3. Add the onion and crumble the cooked bacon into the skillet. Cover and cook, stirring from time to time, until the squash is very limp, so limp it can't get any limper, about 10 minutes.

4. Add the butter and mash the squash right in the pan with a potato masher. Let the squash simmer, uncovered, another 5 to 10 minutes to cook off the extra juices. Taste for seasoning and serve hot.

5 bacon slices

4 medium to large yellow crookneck squash, sliced thin

1 tablespoon salt-and-pepper mix, or 2½ teaspoons salt plus ½ teaspoon ground black pepper

1 medium onion, chopped

2 tablespoons butter

a little
something sweet

HOW WE SOUTHERNERS LOVE OUR SWEETS! They're an everyday delight for many of us. If someone's having a hard time, you might bring them a cake or a pie that you made yourself, a consolation. If someone's died, the family needs sustenance, and while the mac 'n' cheese and fried chicken piles in, it's often the cakes or pies that deliver the most comfort. And at any serious event, like a church supper or a funeral spread, there will be many desserts to choose from, or have a little taste of, so you feel properly looked after.

Even in the Depression, when times were so hard and there was no store-bought sugar, my family had sugar because they grew their own cane and harvested it for syrup. The children could chew on cane stalks and extract a little sweet sugar from the fibers. Aunt Laura remembers that some of the juice for syrup-making was saved and used as a laxative for the children, though it seems like a strange idea that sugar juice could be good for you.

In our community, a good pie or cake maker is all but required to deliver the goods at holiday time, making dozens and dozens of her or his specialty for the entire extended family and their friends. This can easily turn into a small business for those who have the kitchen space. My specialty is Potato Pie, which everyone else calls sweet potato pie, and it seems like I'm baking day and night before Christmas to be sure everyone gets one. But all the desserts in this chapter are good enough to have people begging you for the recipe.

Slap Yo' Mama Coconut Cake
254

Very Red Velvet Cake
258

Key Lime Ice Cream
261

blackberry-raspberry skillet cobbler

This is such a delicious dessert—and it was all an accident. I was making a black-berry cobbler I had high hopes for, and then it turned out I didn't have enough blackberries. But there were some raspberries, so I swapped those in for a quarter of the blackberries. The result was an intense plum-colored fruit filling and a taste that rocked everyone at the table. I tried it all different ways, with different ratios of blackberry to raspberry. But the original accident was the best.

When I make this now, it always reminds me of berry picking up in the country, where we'd get buckets of them. The cobbler looks great in a cast-iron skillet, and even better if you drag a spoon through the batter to make an interesting pattern with the gorgeous berry juice. **SERVES 6 TO 8**

1. To make the filling: Set the oven to 400 degrees.

2. Melt the butter in a 9- or 10-inch cast-iron skillet or a 9-x-12-inch flameproof baking dish. Remove from the heat.

3. Mix the berries with the lemony sugar and spread them out in the bottom of the skillet or baking dish. Let them soften for a couple of minutes in the oven, adding a little water if they seem dry.

4. Meantime, make the batter: Whisk together the flour, sugar, baking powder, and salt in a medium bowl. Stir in the milk—the batter will be thick.

5. Cover the fruit with the batter. It's fine if it doesn't entirely cover the fruit. If you like, pull a spoon through the batter to make a streaky pattern with the juices. Bake the cobbler until the fruit is bubbling up at the edges and a toothpick inserted into the "cobbles" on top comes out clean, about 20 minutes.

6. The cobbler will be too hot to eat when it comes out of the oven. Let it cool for up to 30 minutes, then serve warm in bowls with a pitcher of cream to pour over it at the table.

Filling

- 1 stick (8 tablespoons) butter
- 3 cups blackberries
- 1 cup raspberries
- Grated zest of 1 lemon, mixed with 2 tablespoons sugar

Batter

- 1 cup self-rising flour
- ¾ cup sugar
- 1 teaspoon baking powder
- ¼ teaspoon salt
- ¾ cup milk

- Heavy cream, for serving

TIP

The cobbler is surprisingly good the next day. Reheat it at 350 degrees until the fruit juices begin to bubble up again.

magic peach cobbler

Our Georgia peaches are famous for good reason—you just can't find better, juicier peaches than ours. When they're in season, we love to make this cobbler, and we also make it when peaches are out of season, using canned or frozen peaches (see Tip).

This cobbler gets put together upside down—with the topping on the bottom and the fruit on top. It's magic the way the batter pops right up through the peaches to make a golden brown crust—that's where it gets its name. You want to serve this still warm from the oven, with some good vanilla ice cream. SERVES 6 TO 8

1. To make the filling: Set the oven to 350 degrees.

2. In a medium pot, mix together the water, sugar, and corn syrup and bring to a boil. Add the peaches and cook for 10 minutes over medium heat, stirring a couple of times. Let the peaches cool a bit in the pot, off the heat.

3. Meantime, make the topping: Mix the sugar, flour, and baking powder in a medium bowl. Whisk in the milk–lemon extract blend until most of the lumps are gone.

4. Pour the melted butter into a 13-x-9-inch baking dish; tip the dish around to cover the bottom well. Pour the topping into the baking dish and spread it evenly. Spoon the peaches and their syrup on top, in the middle of the dish. Don't mix the two layers together. Sprinkle the cinnamon evenly all over the top of the cobbler.

5. Bake the cobbler until the crust is golden brown on top, 45 minutes to an hour. Serve warm.

Filling

1½ cups water

½ cup sugar

⅓ cup light corn syrup

5 large peaches, peeled, pitted, and cut into medium slices

Topping

2 cups sugar

1 cup self-rising flour

½ teaspoon baking powder

1 cup whole milk, mixed with ⅛ teaspoon pure lemon extract

3 tablespoons butter, melted

1 tablespoon ground cinnamon

TIP

You can substitute 5 cups defrosted frozen peach slices. You can also use 5 cups canned peaches. Just pour the canned peaches and their syrup right onto the topping batter in the baking dish, without adding any more sugar or corn syrup and without cooking them first.

TIP

Cover leftovers with foil and store in the refrigerator. Heat in a 350-degree oven for 15 to 20 minutes, until the cobbler is hot; the more leftovers you have, the longer the heating time.

talking about peaches

In Georgia, you grow up waiting for the peaches to come in. They start sometime in late May, when you see a few roadside stands advertising tree-ripe peaches. These very early ones are usually from northern Florida, but they can be really good, like the Redcaps I buy from men who picked them the day before.

Our own peaches come in a couple of weeks later, and we look for freestones. I keep an eye out for white ones like Georgia Belles, the ones that never travel and smell the most divine. Then we pounce on them, because you have only about twenty-four hours to enjoy your tree-ripened peach; it can turn brown inside the very next day. You want the ones with the fuzz and the fragrance, and if you can't deal with a whole box of them right away, you can always blanch them for a couple of minutes in a pot of boiling water, peel them, and freeze them whole in plastic bags to enjoy later.

We have peaches all the way into September, so it's about four months of tree-ripened bliss. Freezing them gives us another four months or so. We cook with them, of course, but there's nothing like eating a tree-ripe peach at the moment of its perfection, with the juice running all down your chin and your arms. To me, that's the true taste of the South.

peach shortcake over cream biscuits

You can make this with anything from strawberries to raspberries to mixed berries. When the fruit is perfectly ripe and at its peak of flavor, it's all good. Then these tender biscuits are just right with it, along with some clouds of slightly sweetened whipped cream.

Cream biscuits have to be the easiest ones in the world to make, and they're also among the best. **SERVES 6**

1. To make the biscuits: Set the oven to 425 degrees. Line a baking sheet with parchment paper.

2. Sift the dry ingredients together into a bowl and whisk to mix. Fold in enough cream to make a soft dough you can handle easily. Turn out the dough onto a floured work surface and knead 4 or 5 times.

3. Pat the dough out to a thickness of about ¾ inch and cut into 6 rounds or squares. Dip the biscuits on both sides into the melted butter and arrange them about 1 inch apart on the baking sheet.

4. Bake the biscuits until golden brown, 12 to 14 minutes.

5. To serve: Split the biscuits while they're hot and butter them on the cut sides. Add a sprinkle of white or brown sugar. Set one side of a biscuit buttered face up on a small serving plate and ladle over some peaches. Put the other half of the biscuit on top. Repeat with the remaining biscuits. Pass a big bowl of whipped cream at the table and let everyone help themselves.

Biscuits

- 1 cup all-purpose flour
- 1½ teaspoons baking powder
- ½ teaspoon salt
- 1 teaspoon sugar
- ⅓–½ cup heavy cream, as needed
- 2 tablespoons butter, melted

For Serving

- Soft butter
- White sugar to taste (or brown sugar, if you prefer)
- 2 cups peeled and sliced tree-ripe peaches or other fruit in season (see Tip)
- Sweetened whipped cream (see Box, page 238)

TIP

If you like more peaches than biscuits, you can do open-faced shortcakes, using just half a biscuit for each one.

TIP

If you slice the peaches ahead, stir the juice of ½ lemon into them so they won't turn brown. Lemon juice will also brighten the flavor of berries.

my "potato" pie
(aka sweet potato pie)

I love to watch people's faces when they're first tasting this pie—they just light up. It's sweet but not too sweet, and the spices aren't overpowering. Pumpkin pie is good, but it's nothing special compared to this pie.

This is one of those desserts that takes me back to my roots; it's real soul food, one of the must-have dishes for Christmas and almost any other holiday. In our family, we always called it just plain potato pie, not sweet potato pie, and that's stuck. If I don't make about fifty potato pies for the holidays, my family gets all upset. So I bake them for about three days running, late into the night, to be sure I have enough.

You can use your own piecrust recipe when you make this—or just use your favorite store-bought, which is what I do when I'm making dozens and dozens of them. You can bake the sweet potatoes, which is the easiest way, or boil them, unpeeled.   MAKES 2 PIES

1. Set the oven to 350 degrees. If using homemade piecrusts, put them into the pie pans. Poke holes all over the store-bought or homemade crusts with a fork, even going up the sides—maybe 30 pokes with the fork in each crust. Crimp the edges by hand or with the fork tines. If using store-bought piecrusts, bake them for 5 minutes to set the dough.

2. If you baked the sweet potatoes, split them lengthwise in half and scoop the flesh into a bowl. If you boiled them, cut off the ends of the sweet potatoes and split the skin lengthwise down the top of each potato. Using a fork, gently peel back the skin, remove, and discard. Transfer the potatoes to a bowl.

3. Add the butter to the sweet potatoes and mix on low speed with an electric mixer until the sweet potatoes are well broken up and the butter is incorporated. It's okay if the mixture is a little chunky, and don't worry about the stringy parts—they'll

- 2 (9-inch) store-bought frozen deep-dish piecrusts, partially thawed, in foil pans or homemade crusts
- 6 large sweet potatoes, baked or boiled until soft (see Tips)
- 7 tablespoons butter, softened
- 1⅓ cups sugar
- ⅓ cup self-rising flour
- 1 teaspoon ground cinnamon
- 1 teaspoon grated nutmeg
- 2 large eggs, beaten with a fork
- ½ teaspoon pure vanilla extract
- ½ teaspoon pure lemon extract
- 2 tablespoons evaporated milk
  Sweetened whipped cream (see page 238), for serving (optional)

be left on the beater. Add the remaining ingredients (except the whipped cream) to the sweet potatoes and mix well.

4. Smooth the filling into the crusts—you'll want to fill them right up to the top. Put the pies in the oven and start checking after 30 minutes. The pies will be starting to set when the tops are no longer shiny. After they've been in the oven another 30 minutes or even longer, they'll puff up a bit and then deflate—this means they're done. Remove from the oven and let the pies cool on racks.

5. The pies are very good just the way they are, but some people like them with a little sweetened whipped cream served on the side.

TIPS

• **To bake the sweet potatoes,** scrub them and place them on the middle oven rack with a baking sheet on the rack below to catch any drips. Set the oven to 350 degrees and bake until you can easily pierce the sweet potatoes with a fork, about 50 minutes. **To boil the sweet potatoes,** scrub them and drop into a large pot of water at a rolling boil. Boil for about 50 minutes, or until they can be easily pierced with a fork.

• You can bake the sweet potatoes several days ahead of time (like when you're baking something else at the same temperature). Keep them covered in the refrigerator and bring them to room temperature before you start making the pies.

• For the most delicious sweet potatoes, even if you're peeling them, rub them before baking with fry-meat grease (see page 68) if you have it, or bacon grease.

coconut-pecan pie

This pie, with no corn syrup, is a little lighter than traditional pecan pie, and it's just right after a gigantic holiday meal.

It's fine if you want to use a store-bought piecrust. There are some good ones out there, usually the ones that are already rolled out flat for you. This pie is so easy to put together that there's no point in making a piecrust to complicate things unless you can knock one off in your sleep.   **MAKES 1 PIE**

1. Set the oven at 425 degrees.

2. If using homemade piecrust, put it in the pie pan, fitting it all the way into the corners and trimming the edges if necessary. Lay a sheet of parchment paper or aluminum foil on top and fill with a good layer of dried beans or rice. Bake for 15 minutes.

3. Remove the pie pan from the oven and turn the temperature down to 350 degrees. Gently lift the parchment paper or aluminum foil from the pie pan and save the beans or rice for the next pie you bake.

4. In a large bowl, combine the eggs and yolk and beat well with a fork. Add the two sugars, the butter, lemon juice, and vanilla, beating well with a wooden spoon or silicone spatula to combine. Stir in the coconut flakes and pecans. Pour the filling into the crust.

5. Bake the pie until the filling is set and a golden crust has formed, about 50 minutes. Remove from the oven to cool on a rack.

6. Serve warm or at room temperature, with whipped cream.

1 (9-inch) store-bought frozen piecrust in a foil pan, partially thawed, or homemade crust

4 large eggs plus 1 egg yolk

1 cup white sugar

½ cup dark brown sugar

1 stick (8 tablespoons) butter, melted

2 teaspoons fresh lemon juice

1 teaspoon pure vanilla extract

4 ounces (1 cup) unsweetened coconut flakes, lightly toasted (see Tip)

1 cup coarsely broken pecans

Sweetened whipped cream (see page 238), for serving

TIP

Toasting coconut is easiest in the microwave. Spread the coconut shreds out on a microwave-safe plate. Nuke on high for 1 minute, stir with a fork, and continue in 30-second intervals, stirring well each time. A light toast will take about 2½ minutes, or a little longer. Watch carefully; the coconut can easily burn.

talking about whipped cream

So many Southern desserts are served with whipped cream that the question of how to keep the whipped cream happy, not weepy, comes up often.

- Always use whipping cream, which has more fat than heavy cream and will stay firmer longer. Or just choose the cream with the highest fat content listed on the label.
- Put the beaters and the bowl you're using in the freezer for at least 15 minutes before you start whipping the cream.
- To sweeten 1 cup whipping cream, add 2 tablespoons confectioners' sugar, sifted or sieved. Confectioners' sugar has some cornstarch in it and that will help keep the whipped cream stable.
- Beat the cream to soft peaks and add the sugar, plus vanilla if you're using it, up to 1 teaspoon. Then beat the cream to stiff peaks. You can store the whipped cream in a colander set inside a bowl in the refrigerator for a couple of hours, and any weeping will just drain off into the bowl.
- If you need to keep the whipped cream longer, use gelatin: Mix 1 teaspoon powdered gelatin into 4 teaspoons cold water in a small bowl and let it stand until it gets thick. Put the bowl in the microwave and heat until the gelatin has dissolved, just a few seconds. Let the gelatin cool a bit, then add a few tablespoons of the whipped cream and mix well. Gently mix the gelatin into the rest of the whipped cream, using a rubber spatula to cut and fold it in. This jelled whipped cream will keep for several days in the refrigerator.

better-than-instant banana pudding

People love this banana pudding when I bring a pan of it to share after church. If there's been some bad news, banana pudding, with its layers of bananas and Nilla wafers soaked with vanilla pudding, gives everyone the strength and comfort to deal with it. And it seems to be the ultimate feel-good dessert.

I've made it from scratch and I've made it from instant pudding. I like this one the best of all. It starts with pudding mix (the kind you have to cook), but I doctor it up. If you have kids in the house, they like to help put it together.

SERVES 8 TO 10

1. Heat the milk briefly in a medium saucepan over medium heat. Then add the sour cream, sugar, pudding mix, and vanilla extract, whisking all the time, and whisk until the pudding starts to thicken. Remove from the heat.

2. Slice the bananas. Line a 9-x-13-inch baking dish with half of them. Lay down a layer of the cookies on top of the bananas and stand more cookies up against the sides of the dish. Spoon in half the pudding, then repeat the banana layer, cookie layer, and pudding layer. Crumble the remaining cookies evenly over the top. Cover and refrigerate for a few hours, or overnight.

3. Serve chilled or at room temperature, with whipped cream.

7 cups milk

1 cup sour cream

½ cup sugar

2 (5.1-ounce) packages vanilla pudding (not instant)

2 tablespoons pure vanilla extract

7 large bananas

2 (11-ounce) boxes Nilla wafer cookies

Sweetened whipped cream (see opposite page), for serving

sand tarts

These favorite buttery sugar cookies look a lot like the sand dollars you find lying on the beach. They're crisp, chewy, and thin—and *big*. That's the way we like them. I promise you they won't be around long, but they do keep well in a sealed tin.

The better the butter you use, the better the flavor will be—almost like butterscotch. I like to use Kerrygold, the pure Irish butter, but any good butter will do the trick.

These taste best when you make the dough a day ahead.

MAKES 3 DOZEN COOKIES

1. In a small bowl, whisk together the flour, salt, and baking soda.

2. In a large bowl, with an electric mixer on medium speed, cream the butter and sugar together until light and fluffy. Beat in the vinegar. Add the dry ingredients and mix on low until combined. Cover the dough and refrigerate overnight; if you're short on time, freeze the dough for at least ½ hour (see Tips).

3. Set the oven to 350 degrees and adjust the rack positions to the top and lower thirds. Line two baking sheets with parchment paper.

4. Have ready a small of bowl of water and a small bowl of sugar. Drop the dough by rounded tablespoonfuls onto the cookie sheets, 2 inches apart. Dip the bottom of a glass into the water and then into the sugar and gently flatten each ball with the bottom of the glass to about 3 inches.

5. Bake until the edges of the cookies are golden brown, 12 to 15 minutes, rotating the baking sheets at the halfway mark. Cool completely on a rack. Let the baking sheets cool completely between batches and repeat with the remaining dough.

6. Serve the cookies, or store between sheets of wax paper in a tightly sealed tin.

1½ cups all-purpose flour

1 scant teaspoon salt

½ teaspoon baking soda

2 sticks (½ pound) good creamy butter (I use Kerrygold), softened

1 cup sugar, plus more for topping

½ teaspoon cider vinegar

TIPS

• If the butter in the dough gets too soft, the cookies will spread together on the baking sheet. That's why the trick of refrigerating or freezing the dough before forming the cookies is really important for these. It needs to be just barely softened, so you can work with it.

• If you want to make smaller cookies, just scoop them out smaller and flatten them into smaller cookies, but watch them—they'll bake faster.

orphan one hundred cookies

I got this cookie recipe with the wacky name from my Aunt Laura, who can't remember who gave it to her. So these cookies have no home and no mama. They're chewy, crisp, sandy, rich, buttery, and light, all at the same time. It's hard to stop eating them, so it's a good thing the recipe really does make a hundred cookies. They have a secret ingredient: crunchy Rice Krispies.

MAKES ABOUT 100 COOKIES

1. Set the oven to 350 degrees and adjust the rack positions to the top and lower thirds. Line two baking sheets with parchment paper.

2. Mix together the flour, baking soda, cream of tartar, and salt in a bowl and set aside.

3. In a large bowl, with an electric mixer on medium speed, cream the butter and the two sugars until light and fluffy, 3 to 5 minutes. Add the oil, egg, and vanilla and mix well. On low speed, add the flour mixture and then the remaining ingredients one at a time, beating until everything is mixed in well.

4. Measure out a tablespoon of cookie dough, roll it into a ball, and place it on one of the cookie sheets. Repeat to make more cookies, leaving at least 1 inch between them. Flatten each cookie with the tines of a fork to about ⅛ inch thick.

5. Bake, rotating the sheets at the halfway mark, until the cookies get slightly golden around the edges, 12 to 14 minutes. I like them chewy, so I cook them closer to the 12-minute mark; if you want them crisper, bake for 14 minutes. Don't overbake. Cool the cookies on the pans for 5 minutes, then turn out onto a rack to cool completely. Let the baking sheets cool completely between batches and repeat with the remaining dough.

6. Store in well-sealed tins.

3½ cups all-purpose flour

1 teaspoon baking soda

1 teaspoon cream of tartar

½ teaspoon salt

2 sticks (½ pound) butter, softened

1 cup white sugar

1 cup light brown sugar

1 cup vegetable oil

1 large egg

1 teaspoon pure vanilla extract

1 cup old-fashioned rolled oats

1 cup sweetened coconut flakes

1 cup chopped pecans

2 cups (12 ounces) semisweet chocolate chips

1 cup Rice Krispies cereal

TIPS

• The bigger the cookies are, the chewier and softer they'll be.

• If you want to make smaller cookies, use a teaspoon of cookie dough. The smaller cookies bake much faster; start checking at 9 minutes.

lost-and-found lemon pound cake

Back in the late 1970s, my Aunt Laura was working in a nursing home, and one of her patients, Miss Mary Martin, kept talking about her delicious lemon pound cake. When she was finally well enough to leave and go home, Miss Martin took my aunt's address and promised to send her the recipe.

She did, but she was also struggling with the lingering effects of the stroke she'd suffered, and the recipe was so tangled up that Aunt Laura couldn't figure it out. Years later, when Aunt Laura gave me some family recipes and memorabilia, I found the envelope with the recipe inside.

Of course I had to try to make it, and finally I figured it out. There were some surprises with it: eight eggs, for one thing, and no baking powder, and the sugar was all confectioners' sugar. But there was a direction at the top of the recipe, "Follow step by step," so I was very careful to do that.

And oh, my goodness, what a wonderful cake it is! Feathery-light, rich but not at all heavy, lightly sweet. I'm so grateful to Miss Mary Martin for writing it down, and to Aunt Laura for preserving it. This one is like no other pound cake you've ever eaten. SERVES 16 TO 20

1. Set the oven to 325 degrees. Spray a heavy 10-inch Bundt pan well with baking spray.

2. In a large bowl, with an electric mixer on medium speed, cream the butter until light and fluffy. Slowly add the confectioners' sugar and beat for several minutes, until the mixture is satiny. Add the sour cream, vanilla, and lemon extract, if using, and mix well.

3. Sift the flour and baking soda three times. Add 1 cup of the flour mixture to the butter and mix in well. Then mix in half the egg yolks. Mix in another cup of flour and the remaining yolks. Add the rest of the flour. Don't overmix, or the cake will be tough. Scrape down the sides of the bowl and the beaters and do the final mixing by hand.

1 pound good creamy butter (I used Kerrygold), softened

1 (1-pound) box confectioners' sugar

1 cup sour cream

2 tablespoons pure vanilla extract

1 tablespoon pure lemon extract (optional; see Tip)

3 cups cake flour (Miss Martin specifies Swan's Down)

½ teaspoon baking soda

8 large eggs, separated while cold, then brought to room temperature

Confectioners' sugar, for dusting

continued...

4. In a large bowl, with clean beaters, beat the egg whites to stiff peaks. Gently add the whites to the batter, folding them in with a wooden spoon or a rubber spatula—just barely mix everything together.

5. Scrape the batter evenly into the Bundt pan, rotating the pan as you go and twisting it to level the batter. Rap the pan sharply on the countertop about 30 times, rotating the pan slightly each time, to eliminate any air pockets.

6. Bake for 30 minutes. If the cake is getting too brown on top, turn the oven down to 300 degrees, then test again in 15 minutes. The cake is done when the top springs back when lightly touched and a toothpick inserted into the center comes out clean, about 45 minutes to 1 hour in all.

7. Cool on a rack for 15 minutes, then run a knife around the rim and center tube and invert the cake onto the rack to cool completely.

8. Transfer the cake to a serving plate or a cake stand. Dust with confectioners' sugar.

9. The cake will keep for at least a week at room temperature if it's well wrapped; it also freezes well.

TIP
If you don't have lemon extract, you can use 1 tablespoon fresh lemon juice plus the grated zest of the lemon.

edna's sour cream pound cake with chocolate icing

Edna Blige (the singer Mary J. Blige's cousin) is the paternal grandmother of Keo, my grandson. She's a great baker, and since she loves my potato pie and I love her pound cake, we always swap.

This is like a cross between a traditional pound cake and a sponge cake. It's sweet and tastes good alone and even better with the chocolate icing. **SERVES 8 TO 12**

1. Set the oven to 325 degrees. Spray a 10-inch Bundt pan or tube pan with baking spray.

2. In a large bowl, with an electric mixer on medium speed, cream together the sugar and butter until light and fluffy. Add the eggs one at a time, beating well after each addition. Add the sour cream and vanilla and mix well on low speed. Slowly add the flour, beating just to combine.

3. Scrape the batter into the pan. Bake until the cake is firm to the touch and a thin knife inserted into the center comes out clean, about 1 hour and 20 minutes. Cool on a rack for 15 minutes. Carefully run a knife around the rim and the center tube and invert the cake onto the rack to cool completely.

4. Transfer the cake to a serving plate or cake stand.

5. If you're icing the cake, freeze it for 20 to 30 minutes first. If the icing you're using is too thick to drizzle, either warm it briefly or add a little milk and mix it in well. Spoon a little icing evenly over the top of the cake and let it drizzle down the sides. If it doesn't look right, just frost the whole cake—no one will complain.

3 cups sugar

2 sticks (½ pound) butter, softened

6 large eggs

1 (8-ounce) container sour cream

1½ teaspoons pure vanilla extract

3 cups cake flour, sifted with ¼ teaspoon baking soda

Your favorite chocolate icing (I use the one for Mississippi Mud Cake, page 253)

dorothy lee's five-minute family cake

My soul sister Dorothy Lee has been making this cake since the 1970s, when a friend gave her the recipe. In the years since, she's made a few changes that make it even easier.

Whenever you need a fantastically chocolaty cake that people will go crazy over, here it is, just 5 minutes away from your oven. Now that I know about it, I keep at least one box of the cake mix and the pudding mix in the cupboard so I'm always ready to make it. It's my chocoholic daughter Genie's hands-down favorite cake.

SERVES 12

1. Set the oven to 350 degrees. Spray a 10-inch Bundt pan well with baking spray.

2. Sift together the cake mix and pudding mix into a large bowl. Add the oil, water, and eggs and mix with a fork. Stir in the sour cream and mix well—there shouldn't be any lumps. Scrape all around the bowl with a rubber spatula. Add the chocolate chips and mix well.

3. Spoon the batter evenly into the pan and rap it on the counter to eliminate any air bubbles. Bake for 45 minutes, then check to see if the cake bounces back when you pat it and a toothpick inserted into the center comes out clean. If necessary, bake for 10 to 15 minutes longer.

4. Let the cake cool for 10 minutes on a rack. Carefully run a knife around the rim and center tube and turn the cake out onto the rack to cool completely.

5. Transfer the cake to a serving plate or cake stand. If you want to dress it up, see the Tip. Slice into thick slices to serve.

1 (16.5-ounce) box Duncan Hines Devil's Food Cake Mix

1 (3.8-ounce) package instant chocolate pudding mix

¾ cup vegetable oil

½ cup warm water

4 large eggs, at room temperature, beaten with a fork

Generous ½ cup sour cream

¾ cup chocolate chips

TIP

When it's cool, you can dust this cake with confectioners' sugar to make it more glamorous. Or try the icing for Mississippi Mud Cake (page 253). Warm the icing just enough that you can drizzle it over the cake. Let the icing set up before slicing.

talking about cakes

If you have any hopes of being a good Southern cook, you have to be a great cake baker. In our house, the kids were forbidden to do any bumping and shoving anywhere in the kitchen. Other people I know couldn't even *walk* anywhere near the kitchen when a cake was in the oven.

You do have to pay attention when you're baking a cake, and make sure you're using the right flour, sifting if the recipe wants you to do that, and keeping your eggs and butter at room temperature. But it's not at all mysterious, and you can turn out a fantastic cake that will have people talking for weeks if you stick to the recipe and follow it exactly.

• I think life is too short for the extra work it takes to grease pans with butter, and I think it makes cakes stick. I prefer baking spray, such as Baker's Joy, which does the job in seconds—just be sure to spray at least twice for good coverage. Shortening such as Crisco also works well, and, for luck, add a dusting of Wondra, the superfine flour, tapping out any extra.

• A hand-cranked sifter with a knob on the side will sift much faster and more easily than the kind with the handle that you squeeze. If you don't have a sifter, you can whisk the dry ingredients in a bowl very thoroughly, or push them through a fine-mesh sieve with a cooking spoon.

• Have your eggs and butter at room temperature, and have everything lined up and measured out so you can move smoothly through the recipe.

• In the South, the summer humidity can affect flours, so it's a good idea to keep them tightly sealed in the freezer, where they'll keep fresh for a very long time.

• If I'm going to spread icing on a cake, I first put the cooled cake into the freezer or refrigerator for 20 to 30 minutes. This way you won't have to deal with any crumbs as you're spreading the icing.

• Almost any cake recipe can turn into cupcakes. I always keep cupcake liners on hand. The baking time will be much less, usually about 25 minutes.

• Two important things to own if you're going to become a baker of cakes: a cake stand, which makes the humblest cake look proud, and a cake carrier. Cakes are for celebrating, and that often means they'll be traveling. Carriers ensure that your cake always gets to the party looking swell.

caramel pecan cake

In the South, people just love caramel cake, and this one adds another big favorite, pecans. The cake itself is a little like a pound cake, but lighter. It's really the caramel icing that takes it over the top—when the faces around your table see it dripping down the sides of the cake, there will be a lot of huge smiles.

Because the caramel icing doesn't cover the entire cake, this is not as overwhelming as a lot of caramel cakes—though if you want to, you can frost the entire cake. If you just frost the top, you'll have icing left over; see the Tip. SERVES 12 TO 16

1. To make the cake: Set the oven to 325 degrees. Spray a 10-inch Bundt pan with baking spray.

2. Sift the flour twice with the salt.

3. In a large bowl, with an electric mixer on medium speed, cream the butter. Beat in the sugar and lemon juice and continue beating until the mixture is light and fluffy. Add the eggs one at a time, beating well after each addition. Reduce the mixer speed to low and alternately add the flour and the sour cream to the butter mixture, starting and finishing with the flour. Add the extracts and mix just until they're combined. Turn off the mixer and scrape down the mixer bowl and the beaters. Do a final mixing by hand, then stir in the pecans.

4. Pour the batter into the Bundt pan and rap it on the countertop several times to get rid of any air bubbles. Bake until a toothpick inserted into the center comes out clean, about 1½ hours. Cool the cake in the pan on a rack for 15 minutes.

5. Run a knife around the rim and the center tube and invert the cake onto the rack to cool completely, then transfer to a serving plate or cake stand.

6. To make the icing: In a large saucepan, whisk together 2½ cups of the sugar, the milk, and half-and-half. Add the salt. Bring to a boil over high heat and boil, stirring constantly with

Cake

- 3 cups cake flour
- ¼ teaspoon salt
- 1 stick (8 tablespoons) butter, softened
- 3 cups sugar
- 1 tablespoon fresh lemon juice
- 6 large eggs, at room temperature
- 1 cup sour cream
- 1 teaspoon pure almond extract
- 1 teaspoon pure vanilla extract
- ½ cup chopped pecans

Icing

- 3 cups sugar
- ½ cup milk
- ½ cup half-and-half
- ¼ teaspoon salt
- 1 stick (8 tablespoons) butter, softened
- 1 teaspoon pure vanilla extract
- ½ cup chopped pecans

a wooden spoon, for 3 to 5 minutes, or longer, until the mixture coats the back of the spoon. Remove from the heat.

7. Pour the remaining ½ cup sugar into a large cast-iron skillet or other heavy skillet. Melt the sugar over medium heat and then cook, stirring slowly and constantly with a wooden spoon, until you have a golden brown caramel syrup. The hot sugar can burn you, so be careful!

8. Carefully pour the milk mixture into the skillet—going slowly so it doesn't boil over—and mix well. Pour the icing back into the saucepan, stir in the butter and vanilla, and keep stirring until the icing is cool and thickened.

9. Pour some of the icing carefully over the top of the cake so that you have attractive drips coming evenly down the sides of the cake. (You will have leftover caramel; see the Tip.) Or you can use a thin spatula to frost the entire cake with the caramel. Scatter the pecans over the top of the cake.

10. This cake keeps for several days in a cake keeper.

> **TIP**
>
> You can make caramels out of the leftover icing. Here's how: Line a baking sheet with wax paper and pour the icing on top into a large thin pool. If you have extra pecans, chop them and scatter them evenly over the icing. Let the caramel icing harden slightly, then score it into small squares or rectangles with a sharp knife and let it sit a little longer to firm up. One at a time, carefully pry up the pieces of caramel and roll them into little cylinders. Put each one into a twist of wax paper to store them. These can be hard or chewy; I've had them come out both ways.

mississippi mud cake

This is a fine snacking cake for after school or a picnic—not fancy, but homey and good, a little like a frosted brownie with pecans. And if you keep pecans in the freezer, almost everything else is something usually on hand, so it's a good emergency cake. Another thing I like about this recipe is that you mix the whole thing up in a saucepan and then just pour it into the baking pan.

I ice the cake right in the pan and cut the slices once the frosting is set. Then everyone can help themselves. **SERVES 12**

1. To make the cake: Set the oven to 350 degrees. Butter and flour a 9-x-12-inch baking pan or spray it thoroughly with baking spray.

2. In a large saucepan, melt the butter with the cocoa over medium heat, stirring; don't let it get too hot. Take the pan off the heat and stir in the sugar, then gradually stir in the eggs. Add the flour, baking powder, salt, vanilla, and pecans and mix well.

3. Pour the batter into the pan and rap it on the countertop several times to eliminate air bubbles. Bake until the top of the cake springs back when touched, 35 to 45 minutes. Cool completely on a rack.

4. To make the icing: Mix everything together in a medium bowl, stirring until very smooth. Use the icing immediately; if it sits too long, it will set up and not want to spread.

5. Ice the cake right in the pan. Let the frosting set before cutting the cake into squares and serving. This cake keeps for about 3 days; leave it in the pan and cover tightly with aluminum foil or plastic wrap. Keep it in the refrigerator.

Cake

2 sticks (½ pound) butter

½ cup unsweetened cocoa powder (not Dutch-process)

2 cups sugar

4 large eggs, lightly beaten with a fork

1½ cups all-purpose flour

1 teaspoon baking powder

Pinch of salt

1 teaspoon pure vanilla extract

1½ cups chopped pecans

Icing

1 (1-pound) box confectioners' sugar, sifted

½ cup milk

⅓ cup unsweetened cocoa powder (not Dutch-process)

½ stick (4 tablespoons) butter, softened

slap yo' mama coconut cake

This cake is one of those dangerous ones you can't stop eating, no matter how hard you try. It's light, it's moist, and it has a deep coconut taste, with four different sources of coconut flavor. It's also gorgeous, with its fluffy coconut-flake dress.

SERVES 12

1. **To make the cake:** Set the oven to 350 degrees. Spray two 8-inch round cake pans twice with baking spray.

2. In a medium bowl, whisk the egg whites with the milk and coconut flavoring until frothy. Set aside.

3. In a large bowl, whisk together the cake flour, sugar, baking powder, and salt.

4. In a large bowl, with an electric mixer on medium speed, beat the butter with the cream of coconut for 2 minutes, or until light and fluffy. With the mixer on low, add the dry ingredients in 3 additions, alternating with the wet ingredients in 2 additions. Turn off the mixer, scrape down the sides of the bowl and the beaters, and do a final mixing by hand.

5. Divide the cake batter evenly between the two cake pans. Rap the pans sharply on the countertop several times to get rid of any air bubbles. Bake until the tops are golden brown and a toothpick inserted into the centers of the cakes comes out clean, 35 to 40 minutes. Let the cakes cool in the pans on a rack until cool to the touch, 20 to 30 minutes.

6. Run a knife around the edges of the pans and invert them onto the rack to cool completely, then refrigerate the cakes for 20 to 30 minutes before icing.

7. **Make the filling:** In a large bowl, with an electric mixer on medium speed, cream together the cream cheese, butter, confectioners' sugar, and vanilla until fluffy and spreadable. Stir in the heavy cream until thoroughly blended.

continued...

Cake

5 large egg whites, at room temperature

½ cup milk

1 tablespoon natural coconut flavoring (see Sources, page 263)

3 cups cake flour

2½ cups sugar

1½ teaspoons baking powder

½ teaspoon salt

2 sticks (½ pound) butter, softened

1 cup canned cream of coconut

Filling

6 ounces cream cheese, softened

¾ stick (6 tablespoons) butter, softened

2½ heaped cups confectioners' sugar, sifted

1 teaspoon pure vanilla extract

1 cup heavy cream

8. To make the icing: In a large bowl, with an electric mixer, cream the cream cheese, butter, confectioners' sugar, and coconut flavoring until light and fluffy. Add about 1 tablespoon coconut milk to lighten it, then add more if necessary so it's spreadable.

9. Put one cake layer upside down on a cake plate or cake stand and cover evenly with the filling. Add the second layer right side up. Spread the icing evenly around the sides of the cake and on top; check for any places where you can see through to the cake. Finally, sprinkle the coconut all over the cake as evenly as you can.

10. Let the icing set before serving.

> **TIP**
>
> You can also poke holes all over the unfrosted cake layers with a skewer and brush some juice—I like mango or pineapple—over the tops. The coconut water drained from a real coconut will also help keep the cake moist.

Icing

1 (8-ounce) package cream cheese, softened

1 stick (8 tablespoons) butter, softened

4 cups (1-pound box) confectioners' sugar, sifted

1 teaspoon natural coconut flavoring (see Sources, page 263)

1–3 tablespoons canned coconut milk (mix well before measuring)

1 cup sweetened dried shredded coconut

very red velvet cake

For me, red velvet is the ultimate birthday cake, the one I never get tired of—and I'm not the only one. Mine will knock your socks off, it's such a vibrant magenta color. People just gasp when I cut it. And it's a three-layer cake, so it looks like a Big Deal from the get-go. If you ever need to bring a cake to an event, this is the one to choose.   **SERVES 12 TO 16**

1. To make the cake: Set the oven to 350 degrees and adjust the rack positions to the middle and top third. Spray three 8-inch round cake pans well with baking spray.

2.   Sift the flour with the baking soda.

3. In a large bowl, with an electric mixer on medium speed, beat the eggs well, then beat in the sugar, oil, and vinegar. On low speed, slowly add the flour and beat in well. Add the buttermilk slowly, then the vanilla, and then the food coloring.

4. Pour the batter evenly into the pans and rap them on the countertop several times to eliminate any air bubbles. Bake for 12 minutes, then rotate the pans from shelf to shelf so they bake evenly and bake until the tops spring back when lightly touched, about 25 minutes altogether. Let the cakes cool in the pans on racks for 15 minutes.

5. Run a knife around the sides of the pans and invert the cakes onto the racks to cool completely. Once they're cool, refrigerate the cakes for 20 to 30 minutes to make icing them easier.

6. To make the icing: Combine everything in a medium bowl and mix well until very smooth. It's best to use the icing right away, when it's soft and spreadable.

7. Put one cake layer upside down on a cake plate or cake stand and cover the top evenly with frosting. Add a second layer, right side up, and spread with more frosting. Top with the third layer, right side up, and spread the frosting evenly

Cake

2½ cups cake flour

  ½ teaspoon baking soda

  2 large eggs, at room temperature

1½ cups sugar

1½ cups vegetable oil

  2 tablespoons distilled white vinegar

  1 cup buttermilk

  1 teaspoon pure vanilla extract

  3 tablespoons red food coloring (from two 1-ounce bottles)

Icing

  1 (1-pound) box confectioners' sugar, sifted

  1 (8-ounce) package cream cheese, softened

  1 stick (8 tablespoons) butter, softened

  1 cup chopped pecans

TIP

I sometimes like to mix the pecan bits right into the frosting. Don't worry, they'll stay crisp.

around the sides of the cake and on top; check for any places where you can see through to the cake. Finally, sprinkle the pecans evenly all over the top of the cake.

8. Once the frosting sets, cut into slices to serve. This cake keeps for up to 2 weeks in a cake keeper, but once it's ready, people want to dive right in.

> **TIP**
>
> You can make 18 cupcakes from this recipe. They'll take about 25 minutes to bake.

key lime ice cream

Up in the country, we used to have homemade peach ice cream, which I loved as a child. We had the old-fashioned wooden bucket with a wall of ice and rock salt around the canister, and we all took turns cranking until it got so hard to turn we had to give up. The last one still turning the handle got to lick the dasher when the ice cream was done. I loved that old-fashioned ice cream maker so much that I got the same kind, wooden bucket and all, but mine has an electric motor.

Those round little limes called Key limes seem to be both sweeter and tarter than regular ones. This ice cream has some of that great Key lime pie flavor, but it's a lot more refreshing after a big meal.

Most ice cream bases improve hugely if you let them sit overnight before churning them, and that's true of this one. So be sure to start the recipe the day before you plan to serve it. And don't skip the pinch of salt! **SERVES 4 TO 6**

1. In a large bowl, combine the lime zest, lime juice, and sugar. Slowly whisk in the cream, then the milk and salt. Cover and refrigerate overnight. (If you're using a canister ice cream machine, freeze the canister for at least 24 hours before churning the ice cream.)

2. The next day, churn the ice cream mixture in an ice cream machine. Pack the finished ice cream into a tightly sealed container and let it sit in the freezer for an hour before serving to improve the texture.

2 teaspoons grated Key lime zest

¼ cup plus 1 teaspoon fresh Key lime juice

¾ cup sugar

1 cup heavy cream

1 cup milk

Pinch of salt

TIPS

• Because they're little, Key limes are hard to juice with a regular juicer. An inexpensive Mexican lime squeezer will do the job perfectly.

• If you have leftover limes, they're great to squeeze over fish or anything grilled, and they really brighten up melons.

TIP

If you don't yet have a Microplane fine grater, get one—it makes the job of getting the zest off the limes fun and almost instant. Just move the grater over the fruit as though you were playing a violin, and the zest collects on top.

sources

CANE SYRUP

It's hard to find the real thing, but now I know why old-timers love it so much—it's just so delicious and unlike anything else you've ever tasted. Charles Poirier is making the real thing now in Louisiana, using vintage equipment when he can.

He makes two kinds of cane syrup. Ribbon cane is harvested earlier in the season, and it's a bit like Grade A maple syrup, delicate and light-tasting. Regular cane syrup comes later in the season and is a little more full-bodied, like Grade B maple syrup. Whichever one you want to try—or both—order early, because he sells out quickly. Send him an e-mail at charlespoirier73@gmail.com. Real cane syrup is also available at steensyrup.com.

NATURAL COCONUT FLAVORING

This is available from amazon.com.

CORNMEAL AND GRITS

Stone-ground grits aren't my favorite, but they're good cooked overnight in the oven, especially the ones from Hoppin' John's, which are shipped the day they're ground in the north Georgia mountains. They also sell cornmeal, but not white cornmeal (which is hard to find) and not self-rising. See hoppin'john's.com. Self-rising white cornmeal can be found at loganturnpikemill.com. They ship the day they grind it.

FLOURS

I like to use Martha White self-rising flour for biscuits and other quick breads, and the same brand of all-purpose flour. Martha White is an old Tennessee brand and the company also makes Jim Dandy Quick-Cooking Grits, my favorite. You can check for stores near you where these brands are sold at marthawhite.com. They also do mail-order.

If there's no soft Southern flour such as Martha White available, King Arthur flour sells an excellent soft wheat flour that's self-rising and unbleached. The protein content is 8.5 (see page 75). See kingarthurflour.com.

For cakes, I like to use Swans Down, a very soft fine flour. Check swansdown.com for a store near you.

PEANUTS

Good roasted peanuts can be found at hubspeanuts.com and auntrubyspeanuts.com.

Green peanuts for boiling can be ordered from hardyfarmspeanuts.com in Georgia from August through October.

The Lee Bros. site, boiledpeanuts.com, has boiled peanuts as well as a boil-your-own kit. They also sell grits, cornmeal, and Lowcountry Carolina Gold rice, which dates back to the 1700s—a big treat.

PECANS

Georgia pecans are available every fall from sunnylandfarms.com. Their smaller "junior" pecan halves are especially tasty and great for baking.

RED FIELD PEAS

Anson Mills sells these heirloom Sea Island peas for Hoppin' John in the fall at ansonmills.com. They also sell grits and Carolina Gold rice and lots of other Southern milled grains.

SMOKED SPANISH PAPRIKA

The real thing is Pimenton de La Vera, imported from Spain, usually either sweet or hot. An excellent brand is La Dalia, available from tienda.com or amazon.com. Tienda sells a trio of the paprikas, which includes bittersweet.

CAST-IRON SCRUBBERS

There are a couple of brands of chain-mail stainless steel scrubbers listed on amazon.com. They do a really good job of cleaning cast-iron skillets and pots without removing the seasoning, and they go right into the dishwasher.

GREASE CONTAINER

If you're going to be doing a lot of frying, you'll want to keep the grease for a second or even a third fry (after that, it breaks down and becomes unhealthy). RSVP makes a 6-cup stainless steel pitcher with a strainer on top. It has a lid, so the grease can go directly into the refrigerator and then be reheated on the stovetop right in the pitcher. It's available from amazon.com.

KEY LIME SQUEEZER

You can juice these little limes with a wooden reamer or even a fork, but the easiest way is with a Mexican lime squeezer. Mexican stores usually carry the squeezers, and you can find lots of them listed on amazon.com. To juice the limes, cut them in half and put the cut side down in the press. An enamel-covered metal one is available for a little over $3 at webrestaurantstore.com.

acknowledgments

MY GREATEST THANKS go to God, who is the center of my life and who made this book and so much else possible.

Without my grandmother, Hattie Smith, I might never have learned to cook. She taught me what I know, from how to make coffee to how to make a pot of beans. My father, too, cared a lot about good food and when I was older, he showed me how to find the best things at the market and how to cook them once I got them home.

My old family is long gone. Now my family is my daughter, Genie Charles, and her four sons—Keo Charles and Brandon, Davion, and Tayshun Jones. I love you all so much and give thanks for you every day. You have all been very patient with my frequent trips for work on this book, and you've also been good test subjects for the recipes.

The history of my family would have been lost forever without the help of my Aunt Laura Daniels, the sole remaining survivor of my grandmother's ten children. She provided recipes, counseling, and great stories of the old days, helping me to see the real lives of those who went before me—her parents and her nine siblings.

Someone once asked me how many people would appear in a photograph of my family, and I had to think a bit about it—over eighty people, I finally said. So many of them have helped with this project. All of my sisters—Marilyn Ford, Lillian Jones, Lilliemae Quarterman, and Hattie Ruth Ruff—are fine cooks. My brother, J. J. Smith, gave me some important insight into my parents' lives.

There's a whole new generation of great cooks in the family, especially my niece Delphine Jones, who has been very involved in many aspects of the book, from recipe testing to the photo shoot. My great-nephew Greg Smith was a great help in the kitchen and claimed the recipe for Monkey Bread as his specialty in the process.

My friends have been a godsend. I'm very grateful to my good friend Lisa Jackson, a great cook who also helped with recipes and so much more. Geniver Wade helped me to perfect the meatloaf recipe. Molly Stevens spiffed up the jambalaya recipe. Edna Blige, with whom I trade special dishes, gave me her famous pound cake recipe. Dorothy Lee shared her Five-Minute Family Cake. Teresa Schanck contributed her wise advice.

My close friends Ineata ("Jellyroll") Jones and Felicia Gaines came through for me with amazing help and support. They know my food almost better than I do, and their advice has been very valuable.

My great lawyer and pal Wesley Woolf helped me see that my dream of writing this book and publishing it one day was an actual possibility and then made it happen. The agent we chose, Doe Coover, went far beyond an agent's role to become truly a dear friend.

My editor, Rux Martin, had the same idea about the book I did and made it not only possible and beautiful but also true to my life and my food. Her assistant, Laney Everson, took a special interest in the book and made sure it all went smoothly.

Of course I want to thank Fran McCullough, my writer, who is now my friend and whom I love so dearly. She took my cooking and wrote about it in a way that I couldn't have—but that in the end sounds and tastes just like me. I want to thank her, too, for the respect she showed for my story and for the story of my family. Together we learned so much about my past, and I am grateful for that. I also want to thank Roy Finamore for editing help. I appreciate the beautiful design by Jennifer Beal Davis. Judith Sutton provided astute copyediting.

I can't imagine more beautiful photographs than the ones Robert S. Cooper took, with the help of his assistant, Niduan Zhou, who had arrived from her home in China just three months earlier. Robert is a fellow Savannah native and cook who understands it all.

The recipes came alive in the hands of our food stylist, Erin McDowell, and her assistant, Sarah Daniels. They were beyond amazing, making my food look so good without fussing it up in any way. Two friends, Elizabeth, my lawyer's wife, and Harriet Speer, came through in a pinch with some essential contributions. I am so grateful to both of them. Jessica Quito Perle, the makeup artist for the photos of me in the book, made me glow so that I looked just like myself, only better.

Genealogist Maureen Taylor took the few scraps of clues I had about my family history and turned up vital information, including my parents' marriage certificate, to the great joy of Aunt Laura.

I want to thank Paula Deen for recognizing my skills at the very beginning, giving me a chance, and setting me on a path toward fulfilling my dreams before I even knew I had them. Without Paula, this cookbook wouldn't exist. And Paula was the first to send me flowers and congratulations when she heard this book was becoming a reality. Bobby and Jamie Deen provided a lot of sustaining hugs and kisses over the years. I learned a lot in Paula's kitchen and had many rich, happy days with all my colleagues there.

All these people have blessed me. Thank you all so much!

index

31901056473061